Council of Chief State School Officers
One Massachusetts Avenue, NW, Suite 700
Washington, DC 20001-1431
Phone: 202-336-7000
Fax: 202-371-1766

For more information about the InTASC standards and progressions, please visit www.ccsso.org/intasc. This link includes information on how to order printed copies of this document or download it at no cost.

Suggested Citation:

Council of Chief State School Officers. (2013, April). Interstate Teacher Assessment and Support Consortium InTASC *Model Core Teaching Standards and Learning Progressions for Teachers 1.0: A Resource for Ongoing Teacher Development*. Washington, DC: Author.

Table of Contents

Acknowledgements

InTASC would like to express its sincere appreciation to the National Education Association (NEA), the Educational Testing Service (ETS), and Evaluation Systems group of Pearson for providing the funding for both the standards and progressions projects. Their support has been indispensable to this work being accomplished.

We would also like to offer special thanks to all the InTASC Model Core Teaching Standards Update and Learning Progressions Committee members who enthusiastically volunteered their time and energy to the challenging task of describing what effective teaching across all content areas and grade levels looks like today and how we can support ongoing development of effective teaching practice. InTASC depends upon the support and input from practicing teachers, teacher educators, and other education professionals such as those on our committees to effectively pursue our mission of providing resources to guide education policy.

Finally, InTASC would like to acknowledge and thank the many national education organizations who worked with us by nominating committee members, giving us feedback on our work, and helping us spread the word about these standards and progressions. These organizations include:

- American Association of Colleges for Teacher Education (AACTE)
- American Association of School Administrators (AASA)
- American Federation of Teachers (AFT)
- Association of Teacher Educators (ATE)
- Council for Exceptional Children (CEC)
- Learning Forward
- National Association of Elementary School Principals (NAESP)
- National Association for Gifted Children (NAGC)
- National Association of Secondary School Principals (NASSP)
- National Association of State Boards of Education (NASBE)
- National Association of State Directors of Special Education (NASDSE)
- National Association of State Directors of Teacher Education and Certification (NASDTEC)
- National Board of Professional Teaching Standards (NBPTS)
- National Commission on Teaching and America's Future (NCTAF)
- National Council for Accreditation of Teacher Education (NCATE)
- National Education Association (NEA)
- National Teacher of the Year Program
- National School Boards Association (NSBA)
- Teach for American (TFA)
- Teacher Education Accreditation Council (TEAC)

Introduction

The Council of Chief State School Officers (CCSSO), through its Interstate Teacher Assessment and Support Consortium (InTASC), is pleased to offer this set of combined resources that both define and support ongoing teacher effectiveness to ensure students reach college and career ready standards.

This document includes the *InTASC Model Core Teaching Standards: A Resource for State Dialogue*, which were released in April 2011, and the new *InTASC Learning Progressions for Teachers 1.0: A Resource for Ongoing Teacher Development (2013)*. Together they describe the new vision of teaching needed for today's learners, how teaching practice that is aligned to the new vision develops over time, and what strategies teachers can employ to improve their practice both individually and collectively.

This document is organized as follows: First is an introduction and summary of the *Model Core Teaching Standards*, which describe what the standards are and what they hope to achieve. Second is an introduction to the *Learning Progressions for Teachers*, which describe the increasing complexity and sophistication of teaching practice across a continuum of development. Third are the standards and progressions themselves, with each standard followed by its corresponding learning progression. Lastly, the document includes a glossary, a chart of cross-cutting themes in the standards, and names of committee members who drafted the standards and progressions.

Our hope is that readers find this set of resources useful as we continue to refine our strategies for defining and supporting effective teaching for all learners.

The InTASC Model Core Teaching Standards

The Council of Chief State School Officers (CCSSO), through its Interstate Teacher Assessment and Support Consortium (InTASC), is pleased to offer this set of Model Core Teaching Standards that outline what teachers should know and be able to do to ensure every PK-12 student reaches the goal of being ready to enter college or the workforce in today's world. This "common core" outlines the principles and foundations of teaching practice that cut across all subject areas and grade levels and that all teachers share.

More importantly, these Model Core Teaching Standards articulate what effective teaching and learning looks like in a transformed public education system – one that empowers every learner to take ownership of their learning, that emphasizes the learning of content and application of knowledge and skill to real world problems, that values the differences each learner brings to the learning experience, and that leverages rapidly changing learning environments by recognizing the possibilities they bring to maximize learning and engage learners. A transformed public education system requires a new vision of teaching.

A New Vision of Teaching for Improved Student Achievement

The updating of the core teaching standards was driven not only by new understandings of learners and learning but also by the new imperative that every student can and must achieve high academic standards. Educators are now being held to new levels of accountability for improved student outcomes. These core teaching standards embrace this new emphasis and describe what

> **These standards … describe what effective teaching that leads to improved student achievement looks like.**

effective teaching that leads to improved student achievement looks like. They are based on our best understanding of current research on teaching practice with the acknowledgement that how students learn and strategies for engaging them in learning are evolving more quickly than ever. More research is needed to keep these instructional practices current. These teaching standards promote a new paradigm for delivering education and call for a new infrastructure of support for professionals in the education system. Below are the key themes that run through the updated teaching standards and how they will drive improved student learning.

Personalized Learning for Diverse Learners

The surge in learner diversity means teachers need knowledge and skills to customize learning for learners with a range of individual differences. These differences include students who have disabilities and students who perform above grade level and deserve opportunities to accelerate. Differences also include cultural and linguistic diversity and the specific needs of students for whom English is a new language. Teachers need to recognize that all learners bring to their learning varying experiences, abilities, talents, and prior learning, as well as language, culture, and family and community values that are assets that can be used to promote their learning. To do this effectively, teachers must have a deeper understanding of their own frames of reference (e.g., culture, gender, language, abilities, ways of knowing), the potential biases in these frames, and their impact on expectations for and relationships with learners and their families.

Finally, teachers need to provide multiple approaches to learning for each student. One aspect of the power of technology is that it has made learners both more independent and more collaborative. The core teaching standards give learners a more active role in determining what they learn, how they learn it, and how they can demonstrate their learning. They also encourage learners to interact with peers to accomplish their learning goals. In these ways, the standards embody a vision of teaching that personalizes each learner's experiences while ensuring that every learner achieves to high levels.

A Stronger Focus on Application of Knowledge and Skills

Today's learners need both the academic and global skills and knowledge necessary to navigate the world—attributes and dispositions such as problem solving, curiosity, creativity, innovation, communication, interpersonal skills, the ability to synthesize across disciplines, global awareness, ethics, and technological expertise. CCSSO and the National Governors Association (NGA) have led the work on articulating what learners need to know and be able to do. The Common Core State Standards for English Language Arts and Mathematics, are benchmarked to international standards and include rigorous content and application of knowledge through high-order skills. As states implement these standards, educators throughout the nation will be reexamining what students should know and be able to do throughout their PK–12 education experience.

The core teaching standards describe what teachers should know and be able to do in today's learning context to ensure students reach these learning goals. For example, cross-disciplinary skills (e.g., communication, collaboration, critical thinking, and the use of technology) are woven throughout the teaching standards because of their importance for learners . Additionally, the core teaching standards stress that teachers build literacy and thinking skills across the curriculum, as well as help learners address multiple perspectives in exploring ideas and solving problems. The core teaching standards also address interdisciplinary themes (e.g., financial literacy, civic literacy) and the teacher's ability to design learning experiences that draw upon multiple disciplines.

Improved Assessment Literacy

The current education system treats assessment as a function largely separated from teaching. Yet, teachers are expected to use data to improve instruction and support learner success. The core teaching standards recognize that, to meet this expectation, teachers need to have greater knowledge and skill around how to develop a range of assessments, how to balance use of formative and summative assessment as appropriate, and how to use assessment data to understand each learner's progress, plan and adjust instruction as needed, provide feedback to learners, and document learner progress against standards. In addition, teachers need to know how to make decisions informed by data from a range of assessments, including once-a-year state testing, district benchmark tests several times a year, and ongoing formative and summative assessments at the classroom-level. They should be able to make these decisions both independently and in collaboration with colleagues through a process of ongoing learning and reflection.

A Collaborative Professional Culture

Our current system of education tends to isolate teachers and treat teaching as a solo act. This is counter to what we know about effective teaching today. Just as collaboration among learners improves student learning, we know that collaboration among teachers improves practice. When teachers collectively engage in participatory decision-making, designing lessons, using data, and examining student work, they are able to deliver rigorous and relevant instruction for all students and personalize learning for individual students. The core teaching standards require teachers to open their practice to observation and scrutiny (transparency) and participate in ongoing, embedded professional learning where teachers engage in collective inquiry to improve practice. This includes participating actively as a team member in decision-making processes that include building a shared vision and supportive culture, identifying common goals, and monitoring progress toward those goals. It further includes giving and receiving feedback on practice, examining student work, analyzing data from multiple sources, and taking responsibility for each student's learning.

New Leadership Roles for Teachers and Administrators

These core teaching standards set forth new and higher expectations for teachers, including their role as teacher leaders. Integrated across the standards is the teacher's responsibility for the learning of all students, the expectation that they will see themselves as leaders from the beginning of their career and lead by advocating for each student's needs. The standards also articulate the teacher's obligation to actively investigate and consider new ideas that would improve teaching and learning and advance the profession. Leadership responsibilities are also implicit as teachers participate in the new collaborative culture. Teachers are expected to work with and share responsibility with colleagues, administrators, and school leaders as they work together to improve student learning and teacher working conditions. This includes actively engaging in efforts to build a shared vision and supportive culture within a school or learning environment, establish mutual expectations and ongoing communication with families, and involve the community in meeting common goals.

> **Integrated across the standards is the teacher's responsibility for the learning of all students [and] the expectation that they will see themselves as leaders from the beginning of their career.**

Purpose of this Document

The purpose of the standards is to serve as a resource for states, districts, professional organizations, teacher education programs, teachers, and others as they develop policies and programs to prepare, license, support, evaluate, and reward today's teachers. As noted above, a systemic approach and supportive infrastructure is essential to successful implementation of these standards. In addition to this standards document, CCSSO has also released a complementary policy discussion document that outlines key considerations, recommendations, and cautions for using the standards to inform policy. This paper builds off of CCSSO's Education Workforce white paper (http://www.ccsso.org/intasc), which outlines the chiefs' strategic goals in building an educator development and support system of which these standards are the first step.

In updating the InTASC model standards, efforts were made to ensure they align with other national and state standards documents that were recently revised or released. Specifically, this document has been reviewed to ensure compatibility with the recently-released Common Core State Standards for students in mathematics and English language arts, the National Board for Professional Teaching Standards (NBPTS) accomplished teaching core principles, the National Council for Accreditation of Teacher Education (NCATE) accreditation standards, Learning Forward professional learning standards, the Teacher Leader Model Standards, and the Interstate School Leader Licensure Consortium (ISLLC) 2008 educational leadership policy standards and CCSSO's companion document of performance expectations and indicators for education leaders.

Consistency among all these documents ensures a coherent continuum of expectations for teachers from beginning through accomplished practice, as well as the conditions necessary to support professional growth along this continuum. It also increases the probability of building aligned systems of teacher development and support that begin with recruitment and preparation and run through induction, ongoing professional development, accomplished teaching, and other leadership roles. For a discussion of the implications of these updated standards for teacher policy and practice across the career continuum, please see the companion policy document (http://www.ccsso.org/intasc).

About These Standards

This document is an update to *INTASC's Model Standards for Beginning Teacher Licensing and Development: A Resource for State Dialogue*, which were released in 1992. These standards differ from the original standards in one key respect: These standards are no longer intended only for "beginning" teachers but as professional practice standards, setting one standard for performance that will look different at different developmental stages of the teacher's career. What distinguishes the beginning from the advanced teacher is the degree of sophistication in the application of the knowledge and skills. To reflect this change in emphasis, InTASC removed "new" from its name and now is called the Interstate Teacher Assessment and Support Consortium (InTASC).

> These standards are no longer intended only for "beginning" teachers but as professional practice standards.

Another key point is that these standards maintain the delineation of knowledge, dispositions, and performances as a way to probe the complexity of the teacher's practice. The relationships among the three have been reframed, however, putting performance first—as the aspect that can be observed and assessed in teaching practice. The others were renamed. "Essential knowledge" signals the role of declarative and procedural knowledge as necessary for effective practice and "critical dispositions" indicates that habits of professional action and moral commitments that underlie the performances play a key role in how teachers do, in fact, act in practice.

Vocabulary choice in the document was deliberate to be consistent with the vision being presented. For example, wherever possible "student" was replaced with "learner" because learner implies an active role in learning whereas student could be seen as more passive. Learner also connotes a more informal and accessible role than that of student. Second, "classroom" was replaced with "learning environment" wherever possible to suggest that learning can occur in any number of contexts and outside of traditional brick and mortar buildings that classroom and school imply.

The reader of these standards should keep in mind that while each standard emphasizes a discrete aspect of teaching, teaching and learning are dynamic, integrated and reciprocal processes. Thus, of necessity, the standards overlap and must be taken as a whole in order to convey a complete picture of the acts of teaching and learning.

Also, it is important to keep in mind that indicators are examples of how a teacher might demonstrate each standard. In a performance assessment of teaching covering several days, one would not expect the teacher to demonstrate every indicator—and there may be other indicators that would provide excellent evidence for the standard that the committee did not set forth here. Thus, the indicators are not intended to be a checklist, but rather helpful ways to picture what the standard means.

Next Steps

Standards can serve three different functions. First, they can serve as a "banner," announcing a big picture vision of where we want to go. Second, they can define a specific "bar" or level of performance that must be met. Third, they can articulate the "opportunity to learn" supports that must be in place to ensure a teacher has opportunity to meet the standards. All three are essential to success. These Model Core Teaching Standards are the banner in that their purpose is to describe a new vision of teaching to which we aspire as we work to transform our education system to meet the needs of today's learners. It is a reform document designed to help us see and come to consensus on where it is we want to go.

> **The purpose [of the standards] is to describe a new vision of teaching to which we aspire as we work to transform our education system to meet the needs of today's learners.**

We must build the infrastructure of accountability and support to match the new vision of teaching. Some of this work has already begun. We look forward to working with states and partners in developing consensus around this common core of teaching and moving the standards into practice.

Resources and Research Behind the Standards

The committee drew upon a range of resources in revising the standards. This included key research literature, the work of states who had already updated their standards, and additional key resources such as books and documents related to 21st century learning.

In addition to the above, the committee members themselves—teachers, teacher educators, researchers, state policy leaders—were selected to assure expertise across a range of topics important to the update process. Their expertise was another key resource in the development of the revised standards.

On the issue of research, InTASC commissioned a review of the literature to capture the current evidence base during the standards-writing process. Periodic research updates were given to the committee as the standards work was under way and additional focus areas were added to the review as the committee identified the key ideas grounding its work. The literature review can be found at the InTASC website (www.ccsso.org/intasc) including summary statements of what we know and where there are gaps are in the research. CCSSO considers the research base a work in progress and seeks feedback on the website.

Summary of Updated InTASC Core Teaching Standards

The standards have been grouped into four general categories to help users organize their thinking about the standards:

The Learner and Learning *Category #1*

Teaching begins with the learner. To ensure that each student learns new knowledge and skills, teachers must understand that learning and developmental patterns vary among individuals, that learners bring unique individual differences to the learning process, and that learners need supportive and safe learning environments to thrive. Effective teachers have high expectations for each and every learner and implement developmentally appropriate, challenging learning experiences within a variety of learning environments that help all learners meet high standards and reach their full potential. Teachers do this by combining a base of professional knowledge, including an understanding of how cognitive, linguistic, social, emotional, and physical development occurs, with the recognition that learners are individuals who bring differing personal and family backgrounds, skills, abilities, perspectives, talents and interests. Teachers collaborate with learners, colleagues, school leaders, families, members of the learners' communities, and community organizations to better understand their students and maximize their learning. Teachers promote learners' acceptance of responsibility for their own learning and collaborate with them to ensure the effective design and implementation of both self-directed and collaborative learning.

> Standard #1: Learner Development. The teacher understands how learners grow and develop, recognizing that patterns of learning and development vary individually within and across the cognitive, linguistic, social, emotional, and physical areas, and designs and implements developmentally appropriate and challenging learning experiences.

> Standard #2: Learning Differences. The teacher uses understanding of individual differences and diverse cultures and communities to ensure inclusive learning environments that enable each learner to meet high standards.

> Standard #3: Learning Environments. The teacher works with others to create environments that support individual and collaborative learning, and that encourage positive social interaction, active engagement in learning, and self motivation.

Content *Category #2*

Teachers must have a deep and flexible understanding of their content areas and be able to draw upon content knowledge as they work with learners to access information, apply knowledge in real world settings, and address meaningful issues to assure learner mastery of the content. Today's teachers make content knowledge accessible to learners by using multiple means of communication, including digital media and information technology. They integrate cross-disciplinary skills (e.g., critical thinking, problem solving, creativity, communication) to help learners use content to propose solutions, forge new understandings, solve problems, and imagine possibilities. Finally, teachers make content knowledge relevant to learners by connecting it to local, state, national, and global issues.

> Standard #4: Content Knowledge. The teacher understands the central concepts, tools of inquiry, and structures of the discipline(s) he or she teaches and creates learning experiences that make the discipline accessible and meaningful for learners to assure mastery of the content.

> Standard #5: Application of Content. The teacher understands how to connect concepts and use differing perspectives to engage learners in critical thinking, creativity, and collaborative problem solving related to authentic local and global issues.

Instructional Practice   *Category #3*   *Teaching methods*

Effective instructional practice requires that teachers understand and integrate assessment, planning, and instructional strategies in coordinated and engaging ways. Beginning with their end or goal, teachers first identify student learning objectives and content standards and align assessments to those objectives. Teachers understand how to design, implement and interpret results from a range of formative and summative assessments. This knowledge is integrated into instructional practice so that teachers have access to information that can be used to provide immediate feedback to reinforce student learning and to modify instruction. Planning focuses on using a variety of appropriate and targeted instructional strategies to address diverse ways of learning, to incorporate new technologies to maximize and individualize learning, and to allow learners to take charge of their own learning and do it in creative ways.

> Standard #6: Assessment. The teacher understands and uses multiple methods of assessment to engage learners in their own growth, to monitor learner progress, and to guide the teacher's and learner's decision making.

> Standard #7: Planning for Instruction. The teacher plans instruction that supports every student in meeting rigorous learning goals by drawing upon knowledge of content areas, curriculum, cross-disciplinary skills, and pedagogy, as well as knowledge of learners and the community context.

> Standard #8: Instructional Strategies. The teacher understands and uses a variety of instructional strategies to encourage learners to develop deep understanding of content areas and their connections, and to build skills to apply knowledge in meaningful ways.

Professional Responsibility   *Category #4*

Creating and supporting safe, productive learning environments that result in learners achieving at the highest levels is a teacher's primary responsibility. To do this well, teachers must engage in meaningful and intensive professional learning and self-renewal by regularly examining practice through ongoing study, self-reflection, and collaboration. A cycle of continuous self-improvement is enhanced by leadership, collegial support, and collaboration. Active engagement in professional learning and collaboration results in the discovery and implementation of better practice for the purpose of improved teaching and learning. Teachers also contribute to improving instructional practices that meet learners' needs and accomplish their school's mission and goals. Teachers benefit from and participate in collaboration with learners, families, colleagues, other school professionals, and community members. Teachers demonstrate leadership by modeling ethical behavior, contributing to positive changes in practice, and advancing their profession.

> Standard #9: Professional Learning and Ethical Practice. The teacher engages in ongoing professional learning and uses evidence to continually evaluate his/her practice, particularly the effects of his/her choices and actions on others (learners, families, other professionals, and the community), and adapts practice to meet the needs of each learner.

> Standard #10: Leadership and Collaboration. The teacher seeks appropriate leadership roles and opportunities to take responsibility for student learning, to collaborate with learners, families, colleagues, other school professionals, and community members to ensure learner growth, and to advance the profession.

The InTASC Learning Progressions for Teachers

As a first step toward moving the *InTASC Model Core Teaching Standards* from policy into practice, the Council of Chief State School Officers (CCSSO), through its Interstate Teacher Assessment and Support Consortium (InTASC), crafted *Learning Progressions for Teachers 1.0: A Resource for Ongoing Teacher Development*. These progressions describe the increasing complexity and sophistication of teaching practice for each core standard across three developmental levels. Like the *InTASC Model Core Teaching Standards*, the progressions are focused on describing the key pedagogical strategies needed to get to the new vision of teaching that is essential for successful

> **T**hese progressions describe the increasing complexity and sophistication of teaching practice for each core standard across three developmental levels.

implementation of college- and career-ready standards. This introduction briefly outlines the thinking behind the progressions, how they came to be, and what uses they are intended to serve.

What are the Progressions?

Shortly after release of the *InTASC Model Core Teaching Standards* in April 2011, our state members requested that CCSSO craft rubrics aligned to the standards and so a committee was convened to explore developing such a tool. As the drafting committee consulted with its advisory board and engaged in deep discussion, however, the committee's thinking evolved from a focus on evaluation rubrics to a decision to craft developmental progressions of teaching practice that could be used as a support tool for teacher development. This decision was based on two key findings: First, we recognized that a number of quality evaluation frameworks already existed in the marketplace and we did not want to duplicate efforts. In addition, we found many evaluation systems were missing a robust formative and supportive improvement process to help teachers become more effective. Often systems identify areas for improvement but stop there. Helpful support tools for teacher development are lacking. Second, fairness requires that we articulate a continuum of growth and higher levels of performance with some specificity before holding practitioners accountable for those levels of performance. Teachers should have the opportunity to see what effective practice looks like and how they might get there as a key foundation of any quality evaluation and support system.

Based on these beliefs, and the urgent need for building the capacity of teachers to teach to college- and career- ready standards, the drafting committee took the *InTASC Model Core Teaching Standards* and translated them into learning progressions for teachers that can be used to promote and support their growth. The progressions describe effective teaching with more specificity than the standards, provide guidance about how practice might be improved, and outline possible professional learning experiences to bring about such improvements. What is unique about these progressions is that they make real the components of the new vision of teaching described in the standards and articulate more effective practice based on its key themes (e.g., increased personalization or differentiation of learning, developing learners' higher order thinking skills, promoting cross-disciplinary approaches, collaborating at new levels). In addition, they make concrete suggestions on how a teacher can "shift" from one level to the next. See section below on Movement Across Developmental Levels.

With regard to evaluation, the committee recognizes that the progressions are a type of rubric in that they consist of descriptive criteria against which a teacher or coach can compare performance and make formative judgments to support a teacher's growth. They are not in their current state, however, an evaluation tool in the sense of being tied to processes that have been validated for high stakes summative judgments. A next step in the work will be to explore use of the progressions as the support component with existing state and local frameworks or for development of a new evaluation system and to conduct research on those applications of the progressions.

Key Assumptions Underlying the Progressions

The developmental approach inherent in these progressions rests on several assumptions. In the interest of transparency, those assumptions are outlined here.

Learning and teaching are complex.

Learning and teaching are complex because they involve humans and relationships. We know from research that the teacher/learner connection is the most critical factor in successful learning. In addition to knowing their content, teachers must know their students, how they grow and develop, their preferred ways of learning, their strengths and needs, and their worldview. Teachers must know how to motivate, engage, and inspire their students and do this within a fluid and organic environment that requires constant awareness and adjustment across multiple learners and learning modes, and often with limited resources and support.

Teaching expertise can be learned, develops over time, and is not linear.

Expertise in teaching is knowable and teachable. It can be described, supported by research, demonstrated, experienced, and known. While there is a foundational base of practice with developmental benchmarks along a continuum, not all parts of an individual's performance progress along a continuum at exactly the same pace. Rather, a teacher's particular configuration of performances, knowledge, and dispositions may vary with high performance in some areas and weaker performance in others. Certain professional experiences and supports may spark growth in particular areas and, conversely, changes in context may cause a temporary set-back in skill level until the new context is mastered.

Growth can occur through reflection upon experience, feedback, or individual or group professional learning experiences.

In order to develop their expertise, teachers must become knowledgeable about more effective strategies (know), implement them in a real context (do), gather evidence of learner response to the strategy (use data), reflect upon that evidence (reflect), if possible seek feedback from others like a mentor, coach, peer teacher or observer (get feedback), and then make adjustments (adjust), and repeat the cycle. Teachers must be taught how to work through this cycle and should leave their initial preparation with the skill to reflect on their practice alone and with others, and evaluate their practices against a framework of developmental growth. Intervention is needed when a teacher is unable to reflect or recognize teaching behaviors that should be addressed.

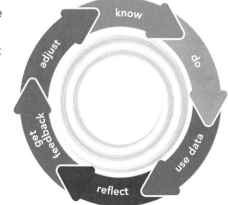

Development depends on context, particularly levels of support.

The effectiveness of a teacher's knowledge and skill varies depending on context and that knowledge and skill may serve them well in one context but less well in another. For instance, a teacher who changes grade levels may find that s/he is at a beginning level in certain skills now needed to teach students at a younger age. A suburban teacher who moves to an urban environment may need different strategies to engage students who have different strengths and needs or who come with different life experiences. The teacher has a reciprocal and iterative relationship with context that needs to be taken into account when supporting their growth and development.

It's about the teaching practice and not about the individual teacher.

The key question is always: What is the impact of practice on the learner?

The focus of these progressions is on the practice of teaching and how to improve practice. The key questions are always these: What is the impact of the practice on the learner? Are the learners engaged? Are they learning, growing, and improving?

Uses of the Progressions

The intended use of these progressions is as a support tool for improving instruction. Their purpose is to provide descriptions of graduated levels of sophistication of teaching practice. Used in this way, they can be a formative assessment tool. The word "assessment" is derived from the Latin *ad sedere*, meaning "to sit down beside." As the etymology implies, assessment (in contrast to evaluation) is primarily concerned with providing guidance and feedback for growth. The progressions provide a pathway and common language from which teachers can talk about their practice. The purpose of the progressions is to generate information for teachers to self-assess against and reflect upon, and for mentors and coaches to use to provide feedback in order to improve professional practice.

The intended use of these progressions is as a support tool for improving instruction.

The progressions can serve as a complement to an evaluation system by being the mechanism through which feedback is provided after an evaluation is conducted and areas for a teacher's professional learning are identified. The progressions can be used for this purpose even if they are not specifically aligned to the evaluation system. This is true because an evaluation system focuses on specific aspects of performance, whereas the progressions address a range of teacher thinking and action that underlies performance or contributes to its effectiveness. The progressions, in effect, become the support system or framework for development through which areas in need of improvement identified through the evaluation can be addressed.

As a tool that provides a common language about how to develop and grow effective teaching practice, the progressions can be used by a range of stakeholders at different stages of a teacher's career. For instance,

- **Preparation program providers and cooperating PK-12 teachers** can use the progressions to inform the preparation curriculum, including what content focus is included and how coursework is sequenced, how experiences during clinical practice should be scaffolded, and what should be included in a "bridge plan" for continued growth for pre-service teachers as they move to in-service and their induction period.

- **Mentors, coaches, and school leaders** can use the progressions to provide feedback to teachers on their performance, including areas for growth and potential learning experiences as part of a continuous improvement process (evaluation feedback and professional development planning), that can inform career advancement or movement to the next stage of practice.

- **State education agency staff and state, district, and local policy makers and staff** can use the progressions to inform what knowledge and skills should be required for licensure, how to develop a tiered licensure system that promotes continued growth, and how to build robust support components of evaluation systems.

- **Teachers and teacher candidates** can use the progressions as an ongoing self-assessment tool to reflect on their individual practice against a framework for development.

Movement Across Developmental Levels

These progressions are intended to describe what movement from basic competence to more complex teaching practice looks like. Generally, this means that the relationship between teacher and learner that defines a teacher's practice moves along a continuum from being more directive (the teacher "directs" what learners do), to more facilitative (the teacher guides learners with some choice and independence), to more collaborative (the teacher works side-by-side with learners who set direction for their own work). Each of these roles requires different and more sophisticated knowledge and skills. Specifically, it means:

> A teacher's practice moves along a continuum from being more directive…to more facilitative… to more collaborative.

- Practice moves toward scaffolding students' learning opportunities so that they are able to assume more responsibility for their learning and make better choices about their learning.

- Practice moves toward helping learners see more connections and relationships and facilitates learning at higher levels of Bloom's taxonomy (revised), including evaluating and creating. These higher order learning skills are what the 2012 Measures of Effective Teaching (MET) research report found is missing in most teachers' practice today and what will be essential practice for us to move toward college-and-career-ready standards. The developmental trend is the teacher's increasing ability to lead learners to their own maximal development.

- Practice moves from a focus on the teacher to a deeper focus on the individual learner, understanding his/her needs, and an increasing ability to differentiate instruction to meet those needs. The focus moves from delivery of instruction to the impact of practice on serving learner needs.

- Practice moves from reliance on the teacher alone to implement strategies to leveraging colleagues and the community to implement and supplement practice, to advocating for learners, and to serving in leadership roles.

- Practice moves from a limited repertoire of strategies to one with greater depth and breadth, including infusing technology in instruction and providing access to resources from around the world.

In addition to describing the nuances of different levels of performance, the progressions begin the process of identifying how a teacher can move from one developmental level to another. In the design of the progressions section, these are called "shifts" in knowledge and skill between levels and include illustrative examples of professional learning that would promote growth toward the shift. Note that these examples are not intended to be exhaustive; rather they suggest professional learning experiences that will move practice to higher levels of performance.

Three key factors are important in focusing professional learning toward individual growth. First, context is a very significant determinant of what kind of professional learning is needed. As noted earlier under the assumptions section, teachers leverage different knowledge and skills depending on the context they are in and the specific configuration of a teacher's strengths and needs will look different in different contexts. Second, while the progressions articulate the specific content of professional learning needed to move from one level to the next, they do not list the many different ways teachers might access that content. Some of those ways are outlined below:

- Personal accessing and processing of media/multimedia including text/audio/video (Web-based or other)

- Independent study and individual reflection

- Collegial study/investigation (Professional Learning Communities (PLCs)/study groups/data analysis groups/Critical Friends groups/book study/action research)

- Mentoring/peer-to-peer coaching /coaching/consulting or collaborating with a specialist

- Structured professional learning through virtual or face-to-face workshops/coursework/webinars

- Actual/virtual observation of effective practices with debriefing and study

- Real world experiences and reflection on the effectiveness of varied teaching and school/community supports

Finally, policy supports are critical so that teachers can effectively access and leverage professional learning opportunities. For instance, providing time during the day to meet or talk with colleagues offers an occasion and incentive for teachers to collaborate. Context and structures in schools must promote the kind of ongoing job-embedded opportunities for continuous growth needed if teachers are to reach the rigorous performance levels outlined in the progressions.

How to Read the Progressions

Several key issues regarding the format of the progressions should be noted. First, because these progressions are a more detailed articulation of the *InTASC Model Core Teaching Standards*, we have included the full standards in this document. To promote ease of use, the teaching standard(s) corresponding to each progression precedes each progression. As noted above, in drafting the progressions we combined the teaching standards' indicators (performances, knowledge, dispositions) into the 3-4 indicators you see for each progression, which capture clusters of related ideas from each standard, and in one case we combined standards (Standards 1 and 2). We cross walked each standard's indicators with the text for each progression and noted in the progressions text, in parentheses, the corresponding teacher standard indicators. We hope this will be a useful reference tool.

Second, each developmental progression moves from left to right, from less to more sophisticated with corresponding numbers 1-3. We did not name the levels of development because we wanted to avoid confining teaching practice to a "box" that labeled performance. Hence, the progressions text is listed in columns with permeable lines between them to denote the fluid nature of development.

Third, the developmental levels are additive as you move across the columns. We used the word "And" between the columns to indicate that the knowledge, skills, and performances in the prior columns come forward into the next one. This indicates that, while there are significant shifts in practice, some parts of prior performance also come forward as appropriate to the work of teaching.

Fourth, as you read across the columns you will note that while some entries in level 1 have a corresponding thread or entry in the adjacent columns, many do not. Each column is intended to be read holistically down and then across as the qualitative change in knowledge and skill may not be exactly parallel across levels, in part because as teaching becomes more complex, elements function in combination or synthesis.

Fifth, as you read down the columns, the shifts underneath the progressions describe in a succinct way the overall qualitative change in knowledge and skill to move from level 1 to 2 and from level 2 to 3. The arrows visually demonstrate this growth and indicate it begins before level 1 (in preparation) and continues beyond level 3 (no cap on accomplishment). Below the shifts are illustrative examples of professional learning experiences that might help a teacher move from one level to the next.

Finally, we included some repetition across standards. This repetition is intentional and strategic. If a specific area is identified for improvement, chances are that the teacher/mentor/coach may very well only go to that standard's progression and indicator without referencing the rest of the document. The repetition ensures they will see a description that covers all the information we considered essential for that indicator or standard's progression.

A First Step

In drafting these progressions, the committee reviewed the research on how teachers grow and develop; we looked at video clips of teachers teaching and working in collegial groups; and we went through a process of "unpacking" the statements in the *InTASC Model Core Teaching Standards*, which included drawing upon our own knowledge bases and experiences as teachers or from working with other teachers to articulate to a finer grain size how teachers grow and develop. The resulting text comes from a combination of research and real life expertise. This work is an extension of the professional consensus around the InTASC standards. It represents our best thinking at this time.

As a beta version, these draft progressions are a foundational jumping off point, if you will, from which we hope to launch a national conversation around how to define and support effective teaching across a continuum of development.

As a beta version, these draft progressions are a foundational jumping off point, if you will, from which we hope to launch a national conversation around how to define and support effective teaching across a continuum of development. They are a work in progress to be explored and revised to improve their usefulness. We are not making any validity claims or claims about generalizability of this work. As brand new work, the progressions need to be studied, refined, and validated. We plan to share the document, work with it, gather feedback from use, and create revised versions. Thus the title is Learning Progressions for Teachers *1.0*. The profession will need to conduct research in order to generate data and robust dialog around the progressions' usefulness as a tool. Our ultimate goal is two-fold: (1) to inspire a research agenda that leads to consensus on what effective teaching looks like and how to develop it; and (2) to build a comprehensive, online, interactive system of support for teachers that includes a rich array of open source resources aligned to these progressions. We hope this framework serves as the first step in achieving those goals.

Standard #1: Learner Development

The teacher understands how learners grow and develop, recognizing that patterns of learning and development vary individually within and across the cognitive, linguistic, social, emotional, and physical areas, and designs and implements developmentally appropriate and challenging learning experiences.

PERFORMANCES

1(a) The teacher regularly assesses individual and group performance in order to design and modify instruction to meet learners' needs in each area of development (cognitive, linguistic, social, emotional, and physical) and scaffolds the next level of development.

1(b) The teacher creates developmentally appropriate instruction that takes into account individual learners' strengths, interests, and needs and that enables each learner to advance and accelerate his/her learning.

1(c) The teacher collaborates with families, communities, colleagues, and other professionals to promote learner growth and development.

ESSENTIAL KNOWLEDGE

1(d) The teacher understands how learning occurs--how learners construct knowledge, acquire skills, and develop disciplined thinking processes--and knows how to use instructional strategies that promote student learning.

1(e) The teacher understands that each learner's cognitive, linguistic, social, emotional, and physical development influences learning and knows how to make instructional decisions that build on learners' strengths and needs.

1(f) The teacher identifies readiness for learning, and understands how development in any one area may affect performance in others.

1(g) The teacher understands the role of language and culture in learning and knows how to modify instruction to make language comprehensible and instruction relevant, accessible, and challenging.

CRITICAL DISPOSITIONS

1(h) The teacher respects learners' differing strengths and needs and is committed to using this information to further each learner's development.

1(i) The teacher is committed to using learners' strengths as a basis for growth, and their misconceptions as opportunities for learning.

1(j) The teacher takes responsibility for promoting learners' growth and development.

1(k) The teacher values the input and contributions of families, colleagues, and other professionals in understanding and supporting each learner's development.

Standard #2: Learning Differences

→ differentiated Instruction

The teacher uses understanding of individual differences and diverse cultures and communities to ensure <u>inclusive learning</u> environments that enable each learner to meet high standards.

→ different learning situations (socially, visually)

PERFORMANCES

2(a) The teacher designs, adapts, and delivers instruction to address each student's diverse learning strengths and needs and creates opportunities for students to demonstrate their learning in different ways.

2(b) The teacher makes appropriate and timely provisions (e.g., pacing for individual rates of growth, task demands, communication, assessment, and response modes) for individual students with particular learning differences or needs.

2(c) The teacher designs instruction to build on learners' prior knowledge and experiences, allowing learners to accelerate as they demonstrate their understandings.

2(d) The teacher brings multiple perspectives to the discussion of content, including attention to learners' personal, family, and community experiences and cultural norms.

2(e) The teacher incorporates tools of language development into planning and instruction, including strategies for making content accessible to English language learners and for evaluating and supporting their development of English proficiency.

2(f) The teacher accesses resources, supports, and specialized assistance and services to meet particular learning differences or needs.

ESSENTIAL KNOWLEDGE

2(g) The teacher understands and identifies differences in approaches to learning and performance and knows how to design instruction that uses each learner's strengths to promote growth.

2(h) The teacher understands students with exceptional needs, including those associated with disabilities and giftedness, and knows how to use strategies and resources to address these needs.

2(i) The teacher knows about second language acquisition processes and knows how to incorporate instructional strategies and resources to support language acquisition.

2(j) The teacher understands that learners bring assets for learning based on their individual experiences, abilities, talents, prior learning, and peer and social group interactions, as well as language, culture, family, and community values.

2(k) The teacher knows how to access information about the values of diverse cultures and communities and how to incorporate learners' experiences, cultures, and community resources into instruction.

CRITICAL DISPOSITIONS

2(l) The teacher believes that all learners can achieve at high levels and persists in helping each learner reach his/her full potential.

2(m) The teacher respects learners as individuals with differing personal and family backgrounds and various skills, abilities, perspectives, talents, and interests.

2(n) The teacher makes learners feel valued and helps them learn to value each other.

2(o) The teacher values diverse languages and dialects and seeks to integrate them into his/her instructional practice to engage students in learning.

Progression for Standards #1 & #2
Learner Development & Learning Differences

The teacher understands how learners grow and develop, recognizing that patterns of learning and development vary individually within and across the cognitive, linguistic, social, emotional, and physical areas, and designs and implements developmentally appropriate and challenging learning experiences.

The teacher uses understanding of individual differences and diverse cultures and communities to ensure inclusive learning environments that enable each learner to meet high standards.

1. The teacher uses understanding of how learners grow and develop (in cognitive, linguistic, social, emotional, and physical areas) to design and implement developmentally appropriate and challenging learning experiences.

1	2	3
	And...	*And...*
Drawing on her/his understanding of child and adolescent development, the teacher observes learners, noting changes and patterns in learners across areas of development, and seeks resources, including from families and colleagues, to adjust teaching. (1a; 7i; 9d)	The teacher builds mental models of variations in typical development based on experience with each learner and uses those models to adjust instruction. (1d)	The teacher uses understanding of the interconnections among different areas of development to find entry point(s) to support learner development. (1e; 1f)
The teacher actively seeks out information about learner interests in order to engage learners in developmentally appropriate learning experiences. (1b)	The teacher incorporates the perspectives of the child and their family/community to integrate new resources and strategies for learner development. (1j; 1k; 9d)	The teacher communicates regularly with families to mutually understand learner development and engages the learner in understanding, analyzing, and communicating their own growth and needs. (1c; 1k)
The teacher engages learners in a variety of learning experiences to capitalize on strengths and build areas of development that are weaker. (1i; 1j)	The teacher seeks and uses in-school and out-of-school resources to support and accelerate each student's learning and development. (1j; 1k; 8n; 9d)	The teacher regularly analyzes and reflects on learners' abilities in order to individualize instruction and take responsibility for the optimal development of each and every learner. (1b)
	The teacher identifies individual learner development and calibrates learning experiences, using an appropriate balance of support and challenge, to move learners toward their next levels of development. (1f)	

Shift to increased ability to:

> Use interactions with learners, families, and communities to better understand variations in development that can guide work with learners

> Use a deep understanding of the ways in which one area of development can affect other areas, in order to personalize learning

Developed through professional learning that will, for example:

EXPAND KNOWLEDGE OF LEARNERS

- ❖ Elicit learner feedback through informal and formal means
- ❖ Consult with colleagues and specialists about particular learner needs
- ❖ Draw on family and community resources through interviews, surveys, home visits, etc.
- ❖ Engage in child study processes to understand an individual child
- ❖ Access online resources such as structured courses on child development, blogs, and podcasts

STRENGTHEN ANALYSIS AND REFLECTION ON PRACTICE

- ❖ Examine practice to see how well it addresses individual learner needs
- ❖ Share practice with others (e.g., invite peers to observe in class, share video
- ❖ of self) and use feedback to better meet learner needs
- ❖ Work with a coach to better understand current practice and make adjustments

BUILD COLLABORATIVE SKILLS TO SUPPORT LEARNERS' COMPLEX DEVELOPMENT

- ❖ Work in professional learning teams to extend knowledge of learner development and probe implications, for example, of linguistic development on cognitive development
- ❖ Work with professional colleagues to design and implement experiences that are responsive to learners' complex developmental needs

BUILD SKILL IN PERSONALIZING AND CUSTOMIZING LEARNING

- ❖ Engage learners in generating ideas for multiple ways to achieve a particular outcome or set of outcomes
- ❖ Engage in a cycle of coaching focused on improving design and practice of personalized learning
- ❖ Examine practice in customizing learning with a critical friend(s)
- ❖ Work collaboratively with professional colleagues to use data to inform the design of individualized instruction

2. The teacher uses understanding of learners' commonalities and individual differences within and across diverse communities to design inclusive learning experiences that enable each learner to meet high standards.

1	2	3
	And...	*And...*
Drawing upon her/his understanding of second language acquisition, exceptional needs, and learners' background knowledge, the teacher observes individual and groups of learners to identify specific needs and responds with individualized support, flexible grouping, and varied learning experiences. (1g; 2b; 2c; 2d; 2e; 2f; 2g; 2h; 2i; 2j; 2l; 2m; 2o)	The teacher continuously expands and deepens his/her understanding of differences and their impact on learning, using interactions with learners and data on learner performance to set goals for individual student learning, to monitor learner progress, and to adjust instruction. (2g; 2h; 2l; 2m)	Across a range of differences, the teacher anticipates and enhances access to challenging learning experiences by providing appropriate guidance, instruction, and resources. (8n; 9d)
Recognizing how diverse learners process information and develop skills, the teacher incorporates multiple approaches to learning that engage a range of learner preferences. (2a; 2d; 2g; 2h; 2m; 8p)	The teacher responds to student learning cues by pacing and adjusting instruction, enhancing access to challenging learning experiences, and making timely provisions (e.g., task demands, communication, assessment, and response modes) for individual learners with particular learning differences or needs. (2a; 2d; 2g; 2h; 2m; 2n; 3r)	The teacher uses a variety of approaches to make concepts clear and provides extensions that engage learners in deepening academic content by connecting it to individual learners' interests, background knowledge, and need for real-world application. (2a; 2b; 2c; 2h; 2l; 2m; 2n)
Using information on learners' language proficiency levels, the teacher incorporates tools of language development into planning and instruction, including strategies for making content and academic language accessible to linguistically diverse learners. (1g; 2b; 2e; 2g; 2i; 2j; 2l; 2m; 2o; 8p)	The teacher engages learners in assessing their strengths and learning preferences and identifies various ways to promote each student's growth (2a; 2b; 2c; 2d; 2j; 2m; 2n)	The teacher challenges each learner by adapting, scaffolding, enriching, and accelerating instruction to facilitate higher order thinking such as analysis, inquiry, and creative expression. (2l; 2m)
The teacher includes multiple perspectives in the presentation and discussion of content that include each learner's personal, family, community, and cultural experiences and norms. (2c; 2d; 2j; 2k; 2m)	Refining her/his understanding of language proficiency levels, the teacher develops a range of supports to assist learners in developing content understanding and language proficiency. (1g; 2e; 2h; 2i; 2o)	The teacher guides learners in taking responsibility for their own learning through individualized goal-setting and progress monitoring. (2l; 2m; 2n)
The teacher applies interventions, modifications, and accommodations based on IEPs, IFSPs, 504s and other legal requirements, seeking advice and support from specialized support staff and families. (2f)	The teacher makes strategic use of learners' primary language to support transfer of language skills and content knowledge. (1g; 2i; 2j; 2m; 2o)	The teacher facilitates learners in taking responsibility for choosing approaches to a learning task that will be effective for them as individuals and produce quality work. (2l; 2m; 2n)
The teacher follows a process, designated by a school or district, for identifying and addressing learner needs (e.g., Response to Intervention) and documents learner progress. (2f; 2g)	The teacher designs learning experiences that facilitate learners' understanding of diverse communities within and outside of their own communities. (2j)	The teacher interacts with language learners to build a common understanding of their language learning experiences and needs, and to collaborate on instructional modifications and strategies to support language learning. (1g; 2e; 2i; 2l; 2n; 2o)
	The teacher adapts instruction and uses modified materials, resources, tools, and technology to address exceptional learner needs, including those associated with disabilities and giftedness. (2a; 2b; 2f; 2g; 2l; 4f; 8n; 8r; 9d)	The teacher integrates diverse languages, dialects, and cultures into instructional practice to build on learners' prior knowledge and experiences and promote the value of multilingual and multicultural perspectives. (1g; 2c; 2e; 2j; 2k; 2n; 2o; 8p)
		The teacher promotes an understanding of inter- and intra-group diversity to facilitate learners' development of cultural competence and build respect across communities. (2j; 2k; 2n; 9e)
		The teacher collaborates with learners, families, and school colleagues to expand the range of resources that address exceptional learning needs and enable learners to meet and exceed high standards. (2f; 2l; 8n; 9d)

Shift to increased ability to:

Deepen knowledge of and apply approaches to adapting instruction to meet the specific needs of individuals and groups of learners	**Anticipate and minimize challenges to learning and increase supports to achieve higher order learning**

Developed through professional learning that will, for example:

EXPAND KNOWLEDGE OF LEARNER DIVERSITY and its implications for adjusting instruction

- ❖ Participate in a structured course of study on second language development and/or cultural competence
- ❖ Interact with parents and local communities to identify resources that can be used to increase relevancy and learner engagement
- ❖ Engage in child study to understand the learner's experience inside and outside of school
- ❖ Consult with colleagues and specialists to deepen understanding of exceptional learner needs and options for adapting instruction

STRENGTHEN ANALYSIS AND REFLECTION ON PRACTICE

- ❖ Examine multiple sources of data to assess the impact of current practice on meeting diverse learners' needs and make adjustments in practice
- ❖ Share practices related to particular groups of learners with colleagues and use feedback to better meet specific learner needs
- ❖ Work with a coach or other colleague to better understand how to adjust practice to meet particular learner needs

BUILD SKILL IN PROBLEM SOLVING to assure the achievement of learner outcomes

- ❖ Work collaboratively to identify and effectively use resources that can support particular learning needs
- ❖ Draw on learner input to structure modes of participation that increase learner interaction, engagement, and autonomy
- ❖ Work with a coach to support the intentional scaffolding of higher order learning across groups of students with particular needs

BUILD SKILL IN PERSONALIZING AND CUSTOMIZING LEARNING

- ❖ Identify particular challenges and use data to systematically address those challenges
- ❖ Work with colleagues to design and test varied supports for high-level achievement for learners with particular needs
- ❖ Share the results of individual or group inquiry to engage professional colleagues, communities, and students in examining ways to support particular groups of learners

Standard #3: Learning Environments

→ Classroom management!!!

The teacher works with others to create environments that support individual and collaborative learning, and that encourage positive social interaction, active engagement in learning, and self motivation.

PERFORMANCES

3(a) The teacher collaborates with learners, families, and colleagues to build a safe, positive learning climate of openness, mutual respect, support, and inquiry.

3(b) The teacher develops learning experiences that engage learners in collaborative and self-directed learning and that extend learner interaction with ideas and people locally and globally.

3(c) The teacher collaborates with learners and colleagues to develop shared values and expectations for respectful interactions, rigorous academic discussions, and individual and group responsibility for quality work.

3(d) The teacher manages the learning environment to actively and equitably engage learners by organizing, allocating, and coordinating the resources of time, space, and learners' attention.

3(e) The teacher uses a variety of methods to engage learners in evaluating the learning environment and collaborates with learners to make appropriate adjustments.

3(f) The teacher communicates verbally and nonverbally in ways that demonstrate respect for and responsiveness to the cultural backgrounds and differing perspectives learners bring to the learning environment.

3(g) The teacher promotes responsible learner use of interactive technologies to extend the possibilities for learning locally and globally.

3(h) The teacher intentionally builds learner capacity to collaborate in face-to-face and virtual environments through applying effective interpersonal communication skills.

ESSENTIAL KNOWLEDGE

3(i) The teacher understands the relationship between motivation and engagement and knows how to design learning experiences using strategies that build learner self-direction and ownership of learning.

3(j) The teacher knows how to help learners work productively and cooperatively with each other to achieve learning goals.

3(k) The teacher knows how to collaborate with learners to establish and monitor elements of a safe and productive learning environment including norms, expectations, routines, and organizational structures.

3(l) The teacher understands how learner diversity can affect communication and knows how to communicate effectively in differing environments.

3(m) The teacher knows how to use technologies and how to guide learners to apply them in appropriate, safe, and effective ways.

CRITICAL DISPOSITIONS

3(n) The teacher is committed to working with learners, colleagues, families, and communities to establish positive and supportive learning environments.

3(o) The teacher values the role of learners in promoting each other's learning and recognizes the importance of peer relationships in establishing a climate of learning.

3(p) The teacher is committed to supporting learners as they participate in decision-making, engage in exploration and invention, work collaboratively and independently, and engage in purposeful learning.

3(q) The teacher seeks to foster respectful communication among all members of the learning community.

3(r) The teacher is a thoughtful and responsive listener and observer.

Progression for Standard #3: Learning Environments

The teacher works with others to create environments that support individual and collaborative learning, and that encourage positive social interaction, active engagement in learning, and self motivation.

1. The teacher collaborates with others to build a positive learning climate marked by respect, rigor, and responsibility.

1	2	3
	And...	*And...*
The teacher sets expectations for the learning environment appropriate to school/district policies and communicates expectations clearly to families. (3n)	The teacher collaborates with learners in setting expectations for a learning climate that include openness, mutual respect, support, and inquiry and in sharing those expectations with learners' families. (3a; 3b; 3c; 3f; 3n; 3r)	The teacher collaborates with learners, families, and colleagues in building a safe, positive learning climate. S/he engages learners, families, and colleagues in expressing mutual expectations for openness, respect, support, and inquiry. (3a; 3c; 3e; 3f; 3l; 3n; 3o; 3r)
The teacher articulates explicit expectations for a safe, positive learning environment, including norms for behavior that include respect for others, as well as responsibility for preparation and completion of work. S/he develops purposeful routines that support these norms. (3a)	The teacher promotes positive peer relationships in support of the learning climate. (3a; 3b; 3j; 3o)	The teacher facilitates the development of school-wide norms and values related to respectful interaction, rigorous discussions, and individual and group responsibility for quality work. (3a; 3e; 3j; 3n; 3o; 3r)
The teacher communicates verbally and nonverbally in ways that demonstrate respect for each learner. (3f; 3r)	The teacher guides the development of classroom norms and values related to respectful interaction, full engagement in discussions, and individual responsibility for quality work. (3e)	The teacher promotes celebration of learning by engaging learners in showcasing their learning and interacting with community members about the quality of their work. (3a; 3n; 10d; 10m)
The teacher is a responsive and supportive listener, seeing the cultural backgrounds and differing perspectives learners bring as assets and resources in the learning environment. (3f; 3r)	The teacher models respectful interaction, verbally and nonverbally, and is responsive to the cultural backgrounds and differing perspectives learners bring to the learning environment. (3a; 3f; 3l; 3n; 3r; 9e)	

Shift to increased ability to:

Facilitate learner contributions to developing a safe, respectful, and engaging learning environment	Collaborate with learners, colleagues, families to foster safe, respectful, and rigorous classroom and school learning environments that promote student responsibility for learning

Developed through professional learning that will, for example:

BUILD SKILLS IN FACILITATING LEARNER INTERACTION

- ❖ Use structured input (e.g., workshops, in-person or online courses, webinars) to learn and practice conflict resolution, restorative discipline, culturally responsive classroom management, etc.
- ❖ Observe colleagues who demonstrate effective elements of respectful classroom environments followed by debriefing
- ❖ Work with colleagues to examine and improve practice that supports full learner engagement

STRENGTHEN ANALYSIS AND REFLECTION ON THE IMPACT OF THE CLASSROOM ENVIRONMENT on student engagement and learning

- ❖ Engage in action research individually or collaboratively to examine the impact of the learning environment on individual responsibility for behavior and quality work
- ❖ Share practice with colleagues to give and receive feedback on strategies to support learner engagement in discussions

BUILD SKILLS AT DEVELOPING LEARNER AUTONOMY AND INTERDEPENDENCE

- ❖ Participate in observations of colleagues who exemplify skills in supporting learners' autonomy and interdependence followed by debriefing and coaching
- ❖ Engage students in learning to use self-assessment strategies to promote individual and group responsibility

BUILD SKILLS IN COLLABORATING with learners, colleagues, and families to assess the rigor of learning environments

- ❖ Use focus groups to get feedback from learners and families on the quality of the learning environment
- ❖ Engage in action research on ways to communicate with learners and families related to meaningful and challenging learning goals.

2. The teacher manages the learning environment to engage learners actively.

1	2	3
	And…	*And…*
The teacher manages the learning environment, organizing, allocating and coordinating resources (e.g., time, space, materials) to promote learner engagement and minimize loss of instructional time. (3d; 8n)	The teacher actively involves learners in managing the learning environment and making full use of instructional time. S/he employs strategies to build learner self-direction and ownership of learning. (3d; 3i; 3p)	The teacher supports learners' independence and self-direction in identifying their learning needs, accessing resources, and using time to accelerate their learning. (3d; 3i; 9d)
The teacher varies learning activities to involve whole group, small group and individual work, to develop a range of learner skills. (3p)	The teacher provides options and resources to engage learners with subject matter and to develop their skills in both collaborative and self-directed learning. (3d; 3i; 3j; 8n; 9d)	The teacher supports learners' growing ability to participate in decision-making, problem solving, exploration, and invention, both suggesting resources and guiding their independent identification of resources. (3p; 9d)
The teacher provides opportunities for learners to use interactive technologies responsibly. (3g; 3m)	The teacher expands the options for responsible use of interactive technologies to extend learning. (3g; 3m)	The teacher collaborates with learners in identifying possibilities for learning locally and globally through responsible use of interactive technologies. (3g; 3m; 9d)

Shift to increased ability to:

Develop learners' self-directed learning skills

Expand learner participation in independent learning and higher order thinking

Developed through professional learning that will, for example:

BUILD SKILL IN ENGAGING LEARNERS TO BECOME MORE SELF-DIRECTED

- ❖ Access resources (books, articles, websites) for gaining knowledge about how to help learners become more self-directed
- ❖ Observe classroom strategies (live or video) for facilitating learner choice and seek coaching to guide own practice of strategies
- ❖ Share practice on learner self-assessment and goal-setting and seek feedback from critical friend(s)
- ❖ Conduct action research on ways to build learners' abilities to use multiple forms of data in ongoing decision-making

DEVELOP EXPERTISE IN APPLYING TECHNOLOGY TO SUPPORT LEARNING

- ❖ Use interactive technologies to expand learner options for mastering content/skills
- ❖ Develop technology options for learners to manage data and direct their own learning
- ❖ Use technology to scaffold content understanding and skill development

BUILD SKILLS IN COLLABORATING WITH LEARNERS AND COLLEAGUES TO ENGAGE IN RIGOROUS, INDEPENDENT, AND INTERDEPENDENT LEARNING

- ❖ Identify and implement interactive technologies to expand learners' experiences
- ❖ Guide learners' independent exploration of local and global resources related to learning goals

STRENGTHEN ANALYSIS AND REFLECTION ON TEACHING FOR HIGHER ORDER THINKING

- ❖ Use data to track learner development of skills related to decision-making and problem-solving.
- ❖ Identify and conduct action research on strategies that support higher order thinking

Standard #4: Content Knowledge

The teacher understands the central concepts, tools of inquiry, and structures of the discipline(s) he or she teaches and creates learning experiences that make these aspects of the discipline accessible and meaningful for learners to assure mastery of the content.

PERFORMANCES

4(a) The teacher effectively uses multiple representations and explanations that capture key ideas in the discipline, guide learners through learning progressions, and promote each learner's achievement of content standards.

4(b) The teacher engages students in learning experiences in the discipline(s) that encourage learners to understand, question, and analyze ideas from diverse perspectives so that they master the content.

4(c) The teacher engages learners in applying methods of inquiry and standards of evidence used in the discipline.

4(d) The teacher stimulates learner reflection on prior content knowledge, links new concepts to familiar concepts, and makes connections to learners' experiences.

4(e) The teacher recognizes learner misconceptions in a discipline that interfere with learning, and creates experiences to build accurate conceptual understanding.

4(f) The teacher evaluates and modifies instructional resources and curriculum materials for their comprehensiveness, accuracy for representing particular concepts in the discipline, and appropriateness for his/her learners.

4(g) The teacher uses supplementary resources and technologies effectively to ensure accessibility and relevance for all learners.

4(h) The teacher creates opportunities for students to learn, practice, and master academic language in their content.

4(i) The teacher accesses school and/or district-based resources to evaluate the learner's content knowledge in their primary language.

ESSENTIAL KNOWLEDGE

4(j) The teacher understands major concepts, assumptions, debates, processes of inquiry, and ways of knowing that are central to the discipline(s) s/he teaches.

4(k) The teacher understands common misconceptions in learning the discipline and how to guide learners to accurate conceptual understanding.

4(l) The teacher knows and uses the academic language of the discipline and knows how to make it accessible to learners.

4(m) The teacher knows how to integrate culturally relevant content to build on learners' background knowledge.

4(n) The teacher has a deep knowledge of student content standards and learning progressions in the discipline(s) s/he teaches.

CRITICAL DISPOSITIONS

4(o) The teacher realizes that content knowledge is not a fixed body of facts but is complex, culturally situated, and ever evolving. S/he keeps abreast of new ideas and understandings in the field.

4(p) The teacher appreciates multiple perspectives within the discipline and facilitates learners' critical analysis of these perspectives.

4(q) The teacher recognizes the potential of bias in his/her representation of the discipline and seeks to appropriately address problems of bias.

4(r) The teacher is committed to work toward each learner's mastery of disciplinary content and skills.

Progression for Standard # 4: Content Knowledge

The teacher understands the central concepts, tools of inquiry, and structures of the discipline(s) he or she teaches and creates learning experiences that make these aspects of the discipline accessible and meaningful for learners to assure mastery of the content.

1. The teacher understands the central concepts, tools of inquiry, and structures of the discipline(s) he or she teaches.

1	2	3
	And…	*And…*
The teacher accurately and effectively communicates concepts, processes and knowledge in the discipline, and uses vocabulary and academic language that is clear, correct and appropriate for learners. (4h; 4j; 4l; 5i)	The teacher seeks out ways to expand or deepen his/her content knowledge and ways of representing it for learners, presenting diverse perspectives to engage learners in understanding, questioning, and analyzing ideas. (4j; 4o; 4r)	The teacher collaborates with others to expand her/his content knowledge in order to keep up with changes in the discipline. (4j; 4o)
The teacher draws upon his/her initial knowledge of common misconceptions in the content area, uses available resources to address them, and consults with colleagues on how to anticipate learner's need for explanations and experiences that create accurate understanding in the content area. (4e; 4k; 4r; 9d)	By analyzing group discourse and learner work, the teacher discovers additional learner misconceptions and uses the processes, vocabulary, and strategic tools of the discipline to build accurate and deep understanding. S/he seeks out or develops resources to fill gaps in learner understanding. (4e; 4k; 4r; 9d)	The teacher evaluates and modifies instructional resources and curriculum materials for their comprehensiveness, accuracy for representing particular concepts in the discipline and appropriateness for his/her learners. (4f; 4n; 4p; 4r; 9d)

Shift to increased ability to:

> **Make content more comprehensible for learners using a broad repertoire of representations of content that promote accurate understanding of content and learners' higher order thinking**

> **Stay current in content knowledge and expand expertise in reviewing instructional materials from the perspectives of both the discipline and individual learner needs**

Developed through professional learning that will, for example:

DEEPEN KNOWLEDGE IN CONTENT AREA

- ❖ Access and process content resources from multiple sources (e.g., books, journals, internet) to build meaningful representations and/or address learner misconceptions
- ❖ Work with teams within and across grade levels to compare representations of content and evaluate their effectiveness for learners
- ❖ Join colleagues in a subject area book study
- ❖ Subscribe to podcasts relevant to content area(s)

STRENGTHEN ANALYSIS AND REFLECTION ON CURRENT CONTENT KNOWLEDGE AND LEARNER NEEDS

- ❖ Identify own content-related strengths and weaknesses and create and implement a professional development plan to enhance content expertise
- ❖ Share content-related practice with a critical friend(s) and use coaching to improve content representation for learner understanding

EXPAND PROFESSIONAL CONNECTIONS IN CONTENT AREA

- ❖ Routinely read journals in the content area
- ❖ Interact with colleagues at conferences sponsored by a professional association to learn and apply new developments in content and content pedagogy

EXPAND KNOWLEDGE OF RESOURCES to support teaching and learning in the content area

- ❖ Integrate new resources into instruction from varied sources (e.g., community members and organizations, other teachers, businesses, learners) that illustrate new developments in the field or applications of content
- ❖ Use descriptive data to analyze and reflect on the effectiveness of resources for building learner mastery of content area concepts

2. The teacher creates learning experiences that make the discipline accessible and meaningful for learners to assure mastery of the content.

1	2	3
	And...	*And...*
The teacher uses multiple representations and explanations that capture key ideas in the discipline, guide learners through learning progressions, and promote each learner's achievement of content standards. (4a; 4j; 4n; 4r; 8e)	The teacher provides multiple representations and explanations of key ideas, with connections to varied learner background knowledge and experiences. S/he evaluates and modifies instructional resources and curriculum materials, when needed, to be more accessible and meaningful for his/her learners. (4a; 4d; 4g; 4p; 4r; 8e; 9d)	The teacher collaborates with colleagues to expand his/her repertoire of representations and explanations of content, including perspectives appropriate to learners from different cultures, linguistic backgrounds, and with varied interests, prior knowledge, and skill levels. (4a; 4m; 4o; 4p; 4r)
The teacher engages learners in applying methods of inquiry used in the discipline. (4c)	The teacher guides learners in critiquing processes and conclusions using standards of evidence appropriate to the discipline. (4b; 4c; 4p)	The teacher facilitates learners' independent use of methods of inquiry and standards of evidence in the discipline. (4b; 4c)
The teacher links new concepts to familiar concepts and helps learners see them in connection to their prior experiences. (4d; 4r)	The teacher stimulates learner reflection on the connection between prior content knowledge and new ideas and concepts. (4d; 4r)	The teacher facilitates learner autonomy in examining new concepts in relationship to their growing base of content knowledge. (4b; 4c)
The teacher models and provides opportunities for learners to understand academic language and to use vocabulary to engage in and express content learning. (4c; 4h; 4o)	The teacher uses a variety of methods to scaffold learner use of academic language allowing learners to engage in and express complex thinking (explanation, analysis, synthesis). (4c; 4h; 4l)	The teacher engages learners in identifying diverse perspectives in discipline-specific inquiry to expand competence in the use of academic language. (4b, 4h)
The teacher consults with other educators to make academic language accessible to learners with different linguistic backgrounds. (4g)		

Shift to increased ability to:

Adapt curriculum materials and instructional strategies to connect with learner backgrounds, experiences, and interests, and to support learner inquiry	Expand and refine purposeful and deliberate adaptation of materials and strategies to meet varied learner needs and promote independent learner inquiry

Developed through professional learning that will, for example:

STRENGETHEN ANALYSIS AND REFLECTION ON USE OF MATERIALS AND RESOURCES

- ❖ Consult with specialists or experienced colleagues to adapt materials and resources for specific learner needs and make further adaptations
- ❖ Use feedback and reflection on learner performance to evaluate effectiveness of materials and strategies

EXPAND KNOWLEDGE OF ACADEMIC KNOWLEDGE IN THE CONTENT AREA

- ❖ Access and process frameworks for building learners' academic language (e.g., journals, books, internet)
- ❖ Analyze language structures for varied functions (e.g., explaining, analyzing) to make vocabulary and language structures comprehensible to learners

EXPAND SKILL IN CREATING AND ADAPTING LEARNING EXPERIENCES

- ❖ Work with colleagues to develop lessons and curriculum units that develop learners' abilities to independently engage in and evaluate their work based on rigorous expectations
- ❖ Co-plan and co-teach with a specialist or experienced teacher to learn a new approach to developing rigorous and relevant learning experiences
- ❖ Try out and use feedback (from colleagues and students) on the use of strategies to scaffold learners' independent use of content area knowledge and processes

BUILD ACTION RESEARCH SKILLS TO IMPROVE PRACTICE THAT LEADS TO LEARNER AUTONOMY

- ❖ Identify resources and strategies tailored for struggling learners
- ❖ Implement strategies and seek feedback from a critical friend(s) on their use with learners
- ❖ Evaluate impact of strategies on student learning and identify possible improvements through examining learner work and eliciting learner feedback

3 r's → rigor, relevance, relationships

Standard #5: Application of Content

Hot → High order of thinking

Thick questions?

The teacher understands how to connect concepts and use differing perspectives to engage learners in critical thinking, creativity, and collaborative problem solving related to authentic local and global issues.

PERFORMANCES

5(a) The teacher develops and implements projects that guide learners in analyzing the complexities of an issue or question using perspectives from varied disciplines and cross-disciplinary skills (e.g., a water quality study that draws upon biology and chemistry to look at factual information and social studies to examine policy implications).

5(b) The teacher engages learners in applying content knowledge to real world problems through the lens of interdisciplinary themes (e.g., financial literacy, environmental literacy).

5(c) The teacher facilitates learners' use of current tools and resources to maximize content learning in varied contexts.

5(d) The teacher engages learners in questioning and challenging assumptions and approaches in order to foster innovation and problem solving in local and global contexts.

5(e) The teacher develops learners' communication skills in disciplinary and interdisciplinary contexts by creating meaningful opportunities to employ a variety of forms of communication that address varied audiences and purposes.

5(f) The teacher engages learners in generating and evaluating new ideas and novel approaches, seeking inventive solutions to problems, and developing original work.

5(g) The teacher facilitates learners' ability to develop diverse social and cultural perspectives that expand their understanding of local and global issues and create novel approaches to solving problems.

5(h) The teacher develops and implements supports for learner literacy development across content areas.

ESSENTIAL KNOWLEDGE

5(i) The teacher understands the ways of knowing in his/her discipline, how it relates to other disciplinary approaches to inquiry, and the strengths and limitations of each approach in addressing problems, issues, and concerns.

5(j) The teacher understands how current interdisciplinary themes (e.g., civic literacy, health literacy, global awareness) connect to the core subjects and knows how to weave those themes into meaningful learning experiences.

5(k) The teacher understands the demands of accessing and managing information as well as how to evaluate issues of ethics and quality related to information and its use.

5(l) The teacher understands how to use digital and interactive technologies for efficiently and effectively achieving specific learning goals.

5(m) The teacher understands critical thinking processes and knows how to help learners develop high level questioning skills to promote their independent learning.

5(n) The teacher understands communication modes and skills as vehicles for learning (e.g., information gathering and processing) across disciplines as well as vehicles for expressing learning.

5(o) The teacher understands creative thinking processes and how to engage learners in producing original work.

5(p) The teacher knows where and how to access resources to build global awareness and understanding, and how to integrate them into the curriculum.

CRITICAL DISPOSITIONS

5(q) The teacher is constantly exploring how to use disciplinary knowledge as a lens to address local and global issues.

5(r) The teacher values knowledge outside his/her own content area and how such knowledge enhances student learning.

5(s) The teacher values flexible learning environments that encourage learner exploration, discovery, and expression across content areas.

Progression for Standard #5: Application of Content

The teacher understands how to connect concepts and use differing perspectives to engage learners in critical thinking, creativity, and collaborative problem solving related to authentic local and global issues.

1. The teacher connects concepts, perspectives from varied disciplines, and interdisciplinary themes to real world problems and issues.

1	2	3
	And...	*And...*
The teacher helps learners see relationships across disciplines by making connections between curriculum materials in a content area and related perspectives from another content area or areas. (5i; 5j)	The teacher collaborates with a colleague(s) in another discipline(s) to create learning experiences that engage learners in working with interdisciplinary themes. S/he guides learners to apply knowledge from more than one discipline to understand a complex concept or set of concepts and/or to address a real world problem or issue. (5j; 5q)	The teacher engages learners in identifying real world problems, issues, or themes they can explore through projects, using their acquired and expanding knowledge and skill in the content areas. (5a; 5j; 5q)
The teacher engages learners in applying content knowledge and skills in authentic contexts. (5b)		The teacher facilitates learners' connections with local and global resources to aid the exploration of their chosen focus. (5l; 9d)

Shift to increased ability to:

> Understand and share multiple disciplinary perspectives to help learners develop more complex understandings of concepts and their application to real world contexts

> Guide learners to develop the strategies needed for personal inquiry and in accessing and using a wide range of resources

Developed through professional learning that will, for example:

DEVELOP KNOWLEDGE AND SKILL IN INTERDISCIPLINARY LEARNING AND REAL-WORLD APPLICATION

- ❖ Access and process media/multi-media resources that demonstrate varied, complex, and applied approaches to learning (e.g., problem-based, inquiry-based, project-based)
- ❖ Observe classrooms or videos of classrooms that model these approaches and debrief practice with colleagues

STRENGTHEN ANALYSIS AND REFLECTION ON THE DESIGN OF INTERDISCIPLINARY LEARNING EXPERIENCES

- ❖ Plan or adapt an interdisciplinary unit, recruit a critical friend or mentor to provide feedback on implementation of that unit, and document what worked and what could be improved
- ❖ Collaborate with a colleague in a different discipline to design a problem-based instructional unit, analyze the contributions and limitations of different disciplines for that unit, and assess learning across the unit

EXPAND KNOWLEDGE AND SKILL IN ENGAGING LEARNERS WITH REAL-WORLD PROBLEMS

- ❖ Access and process resources for improving skills in guiding learners to engage in problem selection, data collection and management, and presentation skills required for real-world problem solving
- ❖ Interact with educators across the globe to build networks of support for own growth in interdisciplinary learning contexts

BUILD ACTION RESEARCH SKILLS ON EFFECTIVE INTERDISCIPLINARY TEACHING AND LEARNING

- ❖ Identify strategies for engaging learners in interdisciplinary inquiry
- ❖ Implement interdisciplinary strategies and seek feedback from a critical friend(s) on their effectiveness with learners
- ❖ Evaluate impact of strategies on student learning and identify possible improvements through examining student work and eliciting student feedback

2. The teacher engages learners in critical thinking, creativity, collaboration, and communication to address authentic local and global issues.

1	2	3
	And…	*And…*
The teacher engages learners in learning and applying the critical thinking skills used in the content area(s). S/he introduces them to the kinds of problems or issues addressed by the content area(s) as well as the local/global contexts for those issues. (5d; 5k; 5m)	The teacher uses problems or questions to guide learner practice in applying the critical thinking skills and other tools in the content area(s). S/he reinforces learners' awareness of how they can use these skills to solve problems or answer questions. (5b; 5d; 5m)	The teacher fosters learners' abilities to independently identify issues or problems of interest in or across content area(s) and engages them in using critical thinking skills in the content area(s) to explore possible solutions, actions or answers. (5b; 5f; 5m; 5o)
The teacher engages learners in developing literacy and communication skills that support learning in the content area(s). S/he helps them recognize the disciplinary expectations for reading different types of text and for writing in specific contexts for targeted purposes and/or audiences and provides practice in both. (5e; 5h; 5n; 8h)	The teacher guides learners in understanding and applying literacy and communication skills in the content area(s) and helps learners reflect on how these skills support their clear communication of understanding of issues and problems in the content area(s). (5e; 5h; 5n; 8h; 8q)	The teacher provides a variety of opportunities for learners to independently and collaboratively apply literacy and communication skills in gathering and analyzing information and in preparing and delivering oral and/or written presentations of their work, marked by clarity, rigor, and suitability for an identified audience. (5e; 5h; 5k; 5n; 5s; 8h; 8q)
The teacher provides opportunities for learners to demonstrate their understanding in unique ways, such as model making, visual illustration and metaphor. (5h)	The teacher supports learners in tailoring communications for different audiences and purposes, consistent with appropriate disciplinary conventions and standards of evidence and argument. (5e; 5h; 5n; 8h; 8q)	The teacher structures options that engage learners in independently and collaboratively focusing on a real world problem or issue, carrying out the design for a solution, and communicating their work. (5a; 5e; 5n; 5o; 5s; 8q)
The teacher guides learners in gathering, organizing and evaluating information and ideas from digital and other resources and from different perspectives. (5c; 5g; 5k; 5l)	The teacher guides learners in developing possible solutions to real world problems through invention, combinations of ideas, or other creative approaches. (5b; 5f; 5o)	The teacher engages learners in independent work to plan and carry out a research project, requiring that they make explicit their evaluation of sources and their reasoning for what they include or omit and presenting their results. (5a; 5k)
The teacher structures interactions among learners and with local and global peers to support and deepen learning. (5p)	The teacher fosters learners' abilities to question and challenge assumptions embedded in source material. (5c; 5d; 5k; 5n)	The teacher fosters learner independence in identifying and accessing local and global people and resources to help them address questions or issues. (5c; 5l; 5s)
	The teacher engages learners in identifying and connecting with local and global people and resources relevant to a topic or question. (5b; 5p)	

Shift to increased ability to:

Build learner awareness of their developing higher order skills and application of those skills in real-world contexts

Foster learner confidence and application of higher order skills in independent and collaborative real-world contexts

Developed through professional learning that will, for example:

BUILD KNOWLEDGE AND SKILL IN GUIDING LEARNERS' TO UNDERSTAND AND APPLY HIGHER ORDER SKILLS

- ❖ Access and use varied resources (courses, workshops, webinars, internet, podcasts, etc.) to support the design and implementation of learning experiences that build critical thinking skills (e.g., Socratic seminar techniques)
- ❖ Observe and debrief with teachers who are successful in supporting learner development of collaborative learning skills (e.g., active listening, talking); implement specific observed strategies and seek feedback on their effectiveness

STRENGTHEN ANALYSIS AND REFLECTION ON ONE'S ABILITY TO USE METACOGNITIVE STRATEGIES

- ❖ Keep a journal documenting the use of metacognitive strategies, analyze those strategies with a critical friend, and refine practice
- ❖ Survey or hold discussions with learners about their increasing awareness of the need to adapt one's communication for real-world audiences
- ❖ Video or audio record lessons aimed at building learner metacognitive strategies and make adjustments based on an analysis of what happened

EXPAND KNOWLEDGE AND SKILL IN PROMOTING LEARNER INDEPENDENCE

- ❖ Form interdisciplinary study groups with colleagues to share resources and debrief practice and to build common strategies to strengthen learner presentation skills and self-assessment skills
- ❖ Engage in collaborative research on ways to support learner creativity through independent and collaborative inquiry projects (e.g., arts-based learning, integration of technology)

BUILD PROFESSIONAL AND COMMUNITY CONNECTIONS TO INCREASE OPTIONS FOR REAL-WORLD APPLICATION

- ❖ Engage in shadowing programs sponsored by local businesses or communities to gain first-hand knowledge of real-world applications of content
- ❖ Use technology to research the potential real-world applications of content in and across disciplines

Standard #6: Assessment

→formative assessment

The teacher understands and uses multiple methods of assessment to engage learners in their own growth, to monitor learner progress, and to guide the teacher's and learner's decision making.

PERFORMANCES

6(a) The teacher balances the use of formative and summative assessment as appropriate to support, verify, and document learning.

6(b) The teacher designs assessments that match learning objectives with assessment methods and minimizes sources of bias that can distort assessment results.

6(c) The teacher works independently and collaboratively to examine test and other performance data to understand each learner's progress and to guide planning.

6(d) The teacher engages learners in understanding and identifying quality work and provides them with effective descriptive feedback to guide their progress toward that work.

6(e) The teacher engages learners in multiple ways of demonstrating knowledge and skill as part of the assessment process.

6(f) The teacher models and structures processes that guide learners in examining their own thinking and learning as well as the performance of others.

6(g) The teacher effectively uses multiple and appropriate types of assessment data to identify each student's learning needs and to develop differentiated learning experiences.

6(h) The teacher prepares all learners for the demands of particular assessment formats and makes appropriate accommodations in assessments or testing conditions, especially for learners with disabilities and language learning needs.

6(i) The teacher continually seeks appropriate ways to employ technology to support assessment practice both to engage learners more fully and to assess and address learner needs.

ESSENTIAL KNOWLEDGE

6(j) The teacher understands the differences between formative and summative applications of assessment and knows how and when to use each.

6(k) The teacher understands the range of types and multiple purposes of assessment and how to design, adapt, or select appropriate assessments to address specific learning goals and individual differences, and to minimize sources of bias.

6(l) The teacher knows how to analyze assessment data to understand patterns and gaps in learning, to guide planning and instruction, and to provide meaningful feedback to all learners.

6(m) The teacher knows when and how to engage learners in analyzing their own assessment results and in helping to set goals for their own learning.

6(n) The teacher understands the positive impact of effective descriptive feedback for learners and knows a variety of strategies for communicating this feedback.

6(o) The teacher knows when and how to evaluate and report learner progress against standards.

6(p) The teacher understands how to prepare learners for assessments and how to make accommodations in assessments and testing conditions, especially for learners with disabilities and language learning needs.

CRITICAL DISPOSITIONS

6(q) The teacher is committed to engaging learners actively in assessment processes and to developing each learner's capacity to review and communicate about their own progress and learning.

6(r) The teacher takes responsibility for aligning instruction and assessment with learning goals.

6(s) The teacher is committed to providing timely and effective descriptive feedback to learners on their progress.

6(t) The teacher is committed to using multiple types of assessment processes to support, verify, and document learning.

6(u) The teacher is committed to making accommodations in assessments and testing conditions, especially for learners with disabilities and language learning needs.

6(v) The teacher is committed to the ethical use of various assessments and assessment data to identify learner strengths and needs to promote learner growth.

Progression for Standard #6: Assessment

The teacher understands and uses multiple methods of assessment to engage learners in their own growth, to monitor learner progress, and to guide the teacher's and learner's decision making.

1. The teacher uses, designs or adapts multiple methods of assessment to document, monitor, and support learner progress appropriate for learning goals and objectives.

1	2	3
	And...	*And...*
The teacher uses, designs or adapts a variety of classroom formative assessments, matching the method with the type of learning objective. (6a; 6b; 6j; 6k; 6r; 6t)	The teacher provides learners with multiple ways to demonstrate performance using contemporary tools and resources. (6a; 6b; 6e; 6g; 6i; 6j; 6o; 6r; 6t)	The teacher uses formative classroom assessments to maximize the development of knowledge, critical thinking, and problem solving skills embedded in learning objectives. (6a; 6c; 6o; 6t)
The teacher uses data from multiple types of assessments to draw conclusions about learner progress toward learning objectives that lead to standards and uses this analysis to guide instruction to meet learner needs. S/he keeps digital and/or other records to support his/her analysis and reporting of learner progress. (6c; 6g; 6j; 6l; 6o; 6t)	The teacher uses data to guide the design of differentiated individual learning experiences and assessments. (6g)	The teacher works individually and with colleagues to gather additional data needed to better understand what is affecting learner progress and to advocate for necessary change. S/he works with colleagues to analyze progress against standards and expand the range of supports for learners with varied learning needs. (6c; 6g; 6l)
The teacher participates in collegial conversations to improve individual and collective instructional practice based on formative and summative assessment data. (6c)	The teacher collaborates with colleagues to analyze performance on formative and summative assessments across groups of learners and engages in joint development of strategies for improving instruction and support to meet standards. (6c; 6l)	The teacher collaborates with others to use summative assessment information to evaluate the effect of the curriculum and instruction on the learner. (6c; 6j; 6l)

Shift to increased ability to:

Use assessment flexibly to expand and deepen understanding of learner performance and determine best supports for continued learner growth	Align assessment techniques to information needed to maximize individual student learning and improve school curriculum and instruction

Developed through professional learning that will, for example:

BUILD KNOWLEDGE AND SKILL IN USING ASSESSMENT EFFECTIVELY

- ❖ Access structured input (e.g., workshops, in-person or online courses, webinars, social media) on matching learning objectives to types of assessments
- ❖ Use protocols to develop strength in using, adapting, or designing assessments to support student learning
- ❖ Use coaching and feedback to improve assessment practice (e.g., vary types of assessments, refine use of data from assessment)

STRENGTHEN ANALYSIS AND REFLECTION ON THE USE OF ASSESSMENT TO SUPPORT STUDENT LEARNING

- ❖ Use grade-level team meetings to share questions and strategies and identify goals for improvement in assessment practice
- ❖ Work with colleagues to examine student assessment data to guide development of needed supports for individuals and groups of learners

EXPAND KNOWLEDGE AND SKILL TO ASSESS HIGHER ORDER SKILLS

- ❖ Learn and use techniques to develop complex performance tasks (e.g., Understanding by Design's GRASPS)
- ❖ Share complex assessments with a critical friend(s) and use feedback to strengthen the design

BUILD SKILLS IN COLLABORATIVE ANALYSIS OF DATA

- ❖ Through work with school or district-level data teams, build skills in identifying target areas of student learning for improvement
- ❖ Access varied resources to develop skill in identifying, organizing, and representing data in ways that are accessible to multiple audiences

2. The teacher uses assessment to engage learners in their own growth.

1	2	3
	And…	*And…*
The teacher engages each learner in examining samples of quality work on the type of assignment being given. S/he provides learners with criteria for the assignment to guide performance. Using these criteria, s/he points outs strengths in performance and offers concrete suggestions for how to improve their work. S/he structures reflection prompts to assist each learner in examining his/her work and making improvements. (6d; 6f; 6n; 6o; 6q; 6r; 6s)	The teacher engages learners in generating criteria for quality work on a particular assignment. S/he identifies key areas in the criteria on which to give individual feedback that will reinforce each learner's strengths and identifies critical next steps for growth. S/he designs learning experiences that help learners apply the feedback and strengthen their performance. (6d; 6f; 6m; 6n; 6o; 6q; 6r; 6s)	The teacher engages learners in giving peers feedback on performance using criteria generated collaboratively. S/he builds learners' metacognitive skills, guiding them to identify how specific elements of the performance contribute to effectiveness and to propose concrete strategies for improvement for themselves and for their peers. (6d; 6f; 6m; 6n; 6q; 6r; 6s)
The teacher makes digital and/or other records of learner performance so that s/he can monitor each learner's progress. (6i)	The teacher makes digital and/or other records of performance available to learners so that they can monitor their progress and identify areas where they need additional practice and support. (6n)	The teacher engages learners in analyzing their own records and work samples with regard to their progress toward learning objectives and to set new goals. (6m; 6n)

Shift to increased ability to:

> **Develop strategies to guide learners in identifying performance criteria and monitoring their own progress**

> **Support learners in use of self and peer assessment and feedback to analyze progress and set goals**

Developed through professional learning that will, for example:

BUILD KNOWLEDGE AND SKILL TO ENGAGE LEARNERS IN THEIR OWN GROWTH

- ❖ Access structured input (e.g., workshops, in-person or online courses, webinars, social media) in developing criteria to guide learners' work as well as to provide feedback to learners
- ❖ Gather (through interaction, internet research, etc.) and use strategies to display data in forms that can guide teacher and learners in monitoring progress (e.g., running records, progress charts)

STRENGTHEN ANALYSIS AND REFLECTION ON PRACTICE TO ENGAGE LEARNERS IN MONITORING PROGRESS

- ❖ Interview learners on their experience of using data to set goals and make adjustments based on insights
- ❖ Share practice and solicit feedback from a critical friend(s) on use of data to engage students in goal-setting

EXPAND KNOWLEDGE AND SKILL WITH ENGAGING LEARNERS IN SELF AND PEER ASSESSMENT

- ❖ Access video exemplars of strategies to develop peer assessment and adapt those strategies to own practice
- ❖ Implement protocols for learner self-assessment and document learner feedback to adapt practice

BUILD COLLABORATION SKILLS ON WAYS TO IMPROVE ASSESSMENT PRACTICE

- ❖ Develop a study group with colleagues to identify resources to support improvement of learner self and peer assessment
- ❖ Facilitate a faculty resource fair on strategies to help students analyze data and set goals

3. The teacher implements assessments in an ethical manner and minimizes bias to enable learners to display the full extent of their learning.

1	2	3
	And...	*And...*
The teacher matches learning goals with classroom assessment methods and gives learners multiple practice assessments to promote growth. (6b; 6j; 6k)	The teacher prepares learners for the content and cognitive demands of assessment formats by engaging them in identifying and applying strategies to address those demands. (6h; 6p; 6q)	The teacher uses multiple assessment methods/modes to scaffold individual learner development toward the learning objectives and to challenge learners to demonstrate their understanding in a variety of ways. (6e; 6e; 6u)
The teacher engages in ethical practice of formal and informal assessment implementing various kinds of assessments in the ways they were intended to be used and accurately interpreting the results. (6j; 6k; 6v)	The teacher modifies classroom assessments and testing conditions appropriately to enable all learners, especially learners with disabilities, language learning needs, and gifts and talents to demonstrate their knowledge and skills. (6e; 6i; 6p; 6t; 6u)	The teacher works with others to minimize bias in assessment practices to ensure that all learners have a variety of opportunities to demonstrate their learning. (6k; 6u; 9e)
The teacher implements required accommodations in assessments and testing conditions for learners with disabilities and language learning needs. (6i; 6k; 6p; 6u)	The teacher identifies and advocates for learners potentially needing modifications or adaptations to be able to demonstrate their learning. (6p; 6t; 6u)	
The teacher differentiates assessments, which may include providing more challenging learning goals for learners who are advanced academically. (6k)		

Shift to increased ability to:

Appropriately prepare, adapt, and/or modify assessment practice ▶▶▶ **Provide multiple supports and experiences for individual learners to develop and demonstrate their learning**

Developed through professional learning that will, for example:

BUILD KNOWLEDGE AND SKILL IN EXAMINING AND MEETING LEARNER NEEDS IN ASSESSMENT CONTEXTS

- ❖ Participate in conversations and decision-making with colleagues and specialists who provide input, guidance, and assistance related to the needs of a particular set of learners to prepare for assessment
- ❖ Seek support from specialists regarding modification of classroom assessment for particular groups of learners
- ❖ Participate in training for modification/adaptation of formal or external assessment

STRENGTHEN ANALYSIS AND REFLECTION ON PRACTICE TO SUPPORT LEARNERS IN ASSESSMENT CONTEXTS

- ❖ Implement strategies to prepare learners with special needs for the demands of assessments and use data to track improvements in learner performance
- ❖ Share modifications of assessments for language learners with a critical friend(s) and use feedback to adjust assessment practice

BUILD NETWORKS OF PROFESSIONAL COLLEAGUES to support ethical assessment practice

- ❖ Participate in professional organizations with others who are concerned with issues of equitable assessment practice
- ❖ Access professional literature related to specific assessment needs of particular groups of learners
- ❖ Establish a listserv to link educators with specialized resources about modification or adaptation of assessment

PROMOTE COLLABORATIVE ACTION RESEARCH

- ❖ Work with colleagues and specialists to apply action research practices to issues in improving assessment to better support learner growth
- ❖ Develop a wiki for the sharing of research questions, processes, and findings related to ethical practice of assessment

Standard #7: Planning for Instruction

The teacher plans instruction that supports every student in meeting rigorous learning goals by drawing upon knowledge of content areas, curriculum, cross-disciplinary skills, and pedagogy, as well as knowledge of learners and the community context.

PERFORMANCES

7(a) The teacher individually and collaboratively selects and creates learning experiences that are appropriate for curriculum goals and content standards, and are relevant to learners

7(b) The teacher plans how to achieve each student's learning goals, choosing appropriate strategies and accommodations, resources, and materials to differentiate instruction for individuals and groups of learners.

7(c) The teacher develops appropriate sequencing of learning experiences and provides multiple ways to demonstrate knowledge and skill.

7(d) The teacher plans for instruction based on formative and summative assessment data, prior learner knowledge, and learner interest.

7(e) The teacher plans collaboratively with professionals who have specialized expertise (e.g., special educators, related service providers, language learning specialists, librarians, media specialists) to design and jointly deliver as appropriate effective learning experiences to meet unique learning needs.

7(f) The teacher evaluates plans in relation to short- and long-range goals and systematically adjusts plans to meet each student's learning needs and enhance learning.

ESSENTIAL KNOWLEDGE

7(g) The teacher understands content and content standards and how these are organized in the curriculum.

7(h) The teacher understands how integrating cross-disciplinary skills in instruction engages learners purposefully in applying content knowledge.

7(i) The teacher understands learning theory, human development, cultural diversity, and individual differences and how these impact ongoing planning.

7(j) The teacher understands the strengths and needs of individual learners and how to plan instruction that is responsive to these strengths and needs.

7(k) The teacher knows a range of evidence-based instructional strategies, resources, and technological tools and how to use them effectively to plan instruction that meets diverse learning needs.

7(l) The teacher knows when and how to adjust plans based on assessment information and learner responses.

7(m) The teacher knows when and how to access resources and collaborate with others to support student learning (e.g., special educators, related service providers, language learner specialists, librarians, media specialists, community organizations).

CRITICAL DISPOSITIONS

7(n) The teacher respects learners' diverse strengths and needs and is committed to using this information to plan effective instruction.

7(o) The teacher values planning as a collegial activity that takes into consideration the input of learners, colleagues, families, and the larger community.

7(p) The teacher takes professional responsibility to use short- and long-term planning as a means of assuring student learning.

7(q) The teacher believes that plans must always be open to adjustment and revision based on learner needs and changing circumstances.

Progression for Standard #7: Planning for Instruction

The teacher plans instruction that supports every student in meeting rigorous learning goals by drawing upon knowledge of content areas, curriculum, cross-disciplinary skills, and pedagogy, as well as knowledge of learners and the community context.

1. The teacher selects, creates, and sequences learning experiences and performance tasks that support learners in reaching rigorous curriculum goals based on content standards and cross-disciplinary skills.

1	2	3
	And...	*And...*
The teacher uses the provided curriculum materials and content standards to identify measurable learning objectives based on target knowledge and skills. (7a; 7g)	The teacher refines learning objectives based on an understanding of student learning progressions and his/her students' development. (7c; 7l; 7q; 9l)	The teacher collaborates with learners in identifying personalized learning objectives to reach long term goals. (7c; 7j; 7m; 7n)
The teacher plans and sequences common learning experiences and performance tasks linked to the learning objectives, and makes content relevant to learners. (7a; 7c; 7k)	The teacher plans a variety of resources and learning experiences that build cross-disciplinary skills and are matched to the experience, needs and interests of individuals and groups. (5a; 7b; 7h; 7m; 7n)	The teacher works with learners to identify pathways to goal achievement using a range of resources, learning experiences, and ways of demonstrating progress toward the learning goal. (7b; 7n)
The teacher identifies learners who need additional support and/or acceleration and designs learning experiences to support their progress. (7j; 7l; 7p)	The teacher plans how s/he will use technology to engage learners in meeting learning objectives. (7b; 7h; 7k; 8o; 8r)	The teacher plans ways to support learners in taking responsibility for identifying learning challenges and using resources to support their progress. (7c; 7n; 9d)
The teacher integrates technology resources into instructional plans. (7k; 7m; 8o; 8r)	The teacher structures time in the plan to work with learners to build prerequisite skills, support steady progress, and/or extend learning. (7c)	The teacher incorporates technology in a variety of innovative ways in planning (e.g., managing learner records, expanding options for learner choice, and documenting performance). (8o; 8r)
	The teacher anticipates specific needs or misconceptions and addresses them by planning scaffolds and/or differentiated instruction. (4e; 7p)	
	The teacher plans learning experiences that allow for learner choice as well as for varied pathways to the same goal. (7b)	

Shift to increased ability to:

Support individual learners to develop deep content understanding and critical learning skills	Expand the role/responsibility of learners to collaborate in planning for their learning

Developed through professional learning that will, for example:

STRENGTHEN ANALYSIS AND REFLECTION ON EXPERIENCE WITH LEARNERS, CURRICULUM, AND INSTRUCTION	**BUILD SKILL IN SUPPORTING LEARNER OWNERSHIP AND RESPONSIBILITY FOR LEARNING**
❖ Systematically analyze student work samples in relationship to curriculum goals in order to adjust planning to meet student needs	❖ Access and use protocols and processes to support learner ownership and responsibility for identifying pathways and resources for learning and get student feedback
❖ Keep annotated notes on lesson plans to guide real-time adjustments and future planning	❖ Observe or participate in team planning of ways to build learner readiness for independent goal-setting, implementing, and monitoring
❖ Work with a mentor and/or invite a colleague to provide feedback on instructional plans	❖ Seek coaching to strengthen ability to work with learners in personalizing learning goals and experiences
EXPAND KNOWLEDGE AND SKILL IN CREATING CHALLENGING LEARNING EXPERIENCES	**STRENGTHEN ANALYSIS AND REFLECTION ON THE IMPACT OF PLANNING** to reach rigorous curriculum goals
❖ Join a study group on the Common Core and/or other college and career ready standards and use the knowledge to adapt instructional plans	❖ Use technology (e.g., clickers, graphs, digital portfolios) to maintain records of learner choice related to ways to customize and personalize learner goals and experiences
❖ Access structured input (e.g., workshops, in-person or online courses, webinars, social media) in the discipline area(s) to build skill in creating challenging learning experiences through the use of technology.	❖ Analyze patterns in learner choice to identify needs for additional resources to support learners in goal attainment
❖ Use grade-level or subject area team meetings to seek feedback on appropriate levels of challenge and support for learners	❖ Engage learners in producing narrative accounts (e.g., blogs, wikis) of meeting challenging learning goals and reflect on ways to support high-level learning

2. The teacher plans instruction based on information from formative and summative assessments as well as other sources and systematically adjusts plans to meet each student's learning needs.

1	2	3
	And...	*And...*
The teacher plans instruction using formative and summative data from digital and/or other records of prior performance together with what s/he knows about learners, including developmental levels, prior learning, and interests. (7d; 7f; 7n)	The teacher aggregates and disaggregates formative and summative data, identifies patterns, and uses these data to inform planning. (7f)	The teacher engages learners in assessing their own learning and uses this as one source of data to individualize and adjust plans. (7f; 7l)
The teacher uses data from formative assessments to identify adjustments in planning. (7d; 7l; 7q)	The teacher uses data from formative assessments to adjust instruction in the moment, to modify planned scaffolds, and/or to provide additional supports/acceleration for individuals and groups of learners. (7d; 7l)	The teacher uses summative assessment data over time to identify and plan for areas where learners typically will need additional supports/ acceleration. (7d; 7l)
The teacher identifies learners with similar strengths and/or needs and groups them for additional supports. (7d; 7l; 7q)		The teacher collaborates with colleagues in using summative data to evaluate instruction and to inform grade level or content area planning at the building or district level. (7f; 7m; 7o)

Shift to increased ability to:

Analyze data and make inferences that assist in differentiating learning and adjusting planning

Use summative and formative data to identify patterns that need to be addressed in planning

Developed through professional learning that will, for example:

BUILD SKILL IN ANALYSIS OF DATA TO GUIDE PLANNING

- ❖ Access structured input (e.g., workshops, in-person or online courses, webinars, social media) to develop approaches and processes for organizing and interpreting data
- ❖ Participate with colleagues in data study to identify implications for instructional planning
- ❖ Collaborate with grade-level or subject-area team to share and seek feedback on plans designed to meet specific learner needs
- ❖ Use protocols developed for the collaborative analysis of data

STRENGTHEN ANALYSIS AND REFLECTION ON USE OF DATA IN PLANNING

- ❖ Work with a mentor or coach to get feedback on ways to use real time classroom data to make adjustments in instruction
- ❖ Use annotated lesson plan notes to learn how to make ongoing adjustments in response to learner needs

EXPAND SKILL IN HIGH-LEVEL DATA ANALYSIS

- ❖ Work with colleagues to examine multiple sources of data over time, looking for patterns that can inform long range planning and the development of learner supports
- ❖ Observe how colleagues use varied formats (e.g., charts, scatterplots, graphs) to engage learners in analyzing their own data and seek coaching to apply similar techniques
- ❖ In grade-level or subject-area teams, use summative data to adjust plans based on curriculum gaps, as well as individual learner needs

BUILD COLLABORATIVE SKILLS TO IMPROVE USE OF DATA IN PLANNING

- ❖ Develop a study group with colleagues to identify resources and processes for high-level data analysis by teachers and learners
- ❖ Contribute to school or district level committees to inform planning at varied levels through examining and interpreting data

3. The teacher plans instruction by collaborating with colleagues, specialists, community resources, families and learners to meet individual learning needs.

1	2	3
	And...	*And...*
The teacher uses learner performance data and his/her knowledge of learners to identify learners who need significant intervention to support or advance learning. S/he seeks assistance from colleagues and specialists to identify resources and refine plans to meet learner needs.(7d; 7e; 7n; 7p)	The teacher uses learner performance data and her/his knowledge of learners to identify specific learning needs of individuals and groups. S/he collaborates with specialists, colleagues, and other learners to plan specific interventions to support or advance learning to meet those needs, thus continually expanding his/her repertoire of strategies. (7m; 7o; 7p)	The teacher uses a wide repertoire of supports in planning to address individualized learner needs and interests in ongoing ways. (7n)
The teacher uses data on learner performance over time to inform planning, making adjustments for recurring learning needs. (7f; 7p)	The teacher works collaboratively with families to plan ways to meet the needs of learners, incorporating and using assets in the family and community that support learner goals. (7e; 7m; 7o)	The teacher engages learners as partners in planning, identifying the learning pathways that will help them pursue challenging goals. (7e; 7o)
The teacher uses information from informal interactions with families to adjust his/her plans and to incorporate home-based resources to provide further support. (7o; 7q)		The teacher collaborates with a broad range of colleagues, specialists, and community members to understand and address each student's learning needs (e.g., developmental, exceptional, linguistic). S/he employs cultural resources and varied community practices and perspectives to build a web of support to meet learners' needs. (7e; 7m; 7o; 9l)

Shift to increased ability to:

Use a range of inputs and resources in planning	Personalize learning through engagement of learners and learners' communities

Developed through professional learning that will, for example:

BUILD KNOWLEDGE OF RESOURCES FOR PLANNING

- ❖ Solicit feedback from colleagues, coaches, and mentors on using data to identify targeted resources for planning
- ❖ Access structured input (e.g., workshops, in-person or online courses, webinars, social media) to find varied resources and strategies to meet specific learning needs

BUILD COLLABORATION SKILLS WITH FAMILIES AS PARTNERS IN PLANNING

- ❖ Use or create opportunities to connect with families (e.g., home visits, community events, classroom celebrations) in support of increasing relevancy in planning
- ❖ Interview community members or identify a community mentor who can help make connections to community resources for planning

EXPAND KNOWLEDGE AND SKILL OF RESOURCES FOR PLANNING

- ❖ Seek coaching to develop deeper understanding and use of cultural and community resources that can be integrated in planning
- ❖ Work with a mentor or colleague(s) to develop and apply for grant(s) to support increased collaboration with parents and community members in planning relevant and rigorous curriculum and co-curricular activities

BUILD PROFESSIONAL COMMUNITY TO SHARE RESOURCES

- ❖ Use technology to share, analyze, and reflect on resources that can support learners in attaining high goals
- ❖ Build a virtual community (e.g., website, wiki) to support the sharing of resources with professional colleagues

Standard #8: Instructional Strategies

The teacher understands and uses a variety of instructional strategies to encourage learners to develop deep understanding of content areas and their connections, and to build skills to apply knowledge in meaningful ways.

PERFORMANCES

8(a) The teacher uses appropriate strategies and resources to adapt instruction to the needs of individuals and groups of learners.

8(b) The teacher continuously monitors student learning, engages learners in assessing their progress, and adjusts instruction in response to student learning needs.

8(c) The teacher collaborates with learners to design and implement relevant learning experiences, identify their strengths, and access family and community resources to develop their areas of interest.

8(d) The teacher varies his/her role in the instructional process (e.g., instructor, facilitator, coach, audience) in relation to the content and purposes of instruction and the needs of learners.

8(e) The teacher provides multiple models and representations of concepts and skills with opportunities for learners to demonstrate their knowledge through a variety of products and performances.

8(f) The teacher engages all learners in developing higher order questioning skills and metacognitive processes.

8(g) The teacher engages learners in using a range of learning skills and technology tools to access, interpret, evaluate, and apply information.

8(h) The teacher uses a variety of instructional strategies to support and expand learners' communication through speaking, listening, reading, writing, and other modes.

8(i) The teacher asks questions to stimulate discussion that serves different purposes (e.g., probing for learner understanding, helping learners articulate their ideas and thinking processes, stimulating curiosity, and helping learners to question).

ESSENTIAL KNOWLEDGE

8(j) The teacher understands the cognitive processes associated with various kinds of learning (e.g., critical and creative thinking, problem framing and problem solving, invention, memorization and recall) and how these processes can be stimulated.

8(k) The teacher knows how to apply a range of developmentally, culturally, and linguistically appropriate instructional strategies to achieve learning goals.

8(l) The teacher knows when and how to use appropriate strategies to differentiate instruction and engage all learners in complex thinking and meaningful tasks.

8(m) The teacher understands how multiple forms of communication (oral, written, nonverbal, digital, visual) convey ideas, foster self expression, and build relationships.

8(n) The teacher knows how to use a wide variety of resources, including human and technological, to engage students in learning.

8(o) The teacher understands how content and skill development can be supported by media and technology and knows how to evaluate these resources for quality, accuracy, and effectiveness.

CRITICAL DISPOSITIONS

8(p) The teacher is committed to deepening awareness and understanding the strengths and needs of diverse learners when planning and adjusting instruction.

8(q) The teacher values the variety of ways people communicate and encourages learners to develop and use multiple forms of communication.

8(r) The teacher is committed to exploring how the use of new and emerging technologies can support and promote student learning.

8(s) The teacher values flexibility and reciprocity in the teaching process as necessary for adapting instruction to learner responses, ideas, and needs.

Progression for Standard #8: Instructional Strategies

The teacher understands and uses a variety of instructional strategies to encourage learners to develop deep understanding of content areas and their connections, and to build skills to apply knowledge in meaningful ways.

1. The teacher understands and uses a variety of instructional strategies and makes learning accessible to all learners.

1	2	3
	And...	*And...*
The teacher directs students' learning experiences through instructional strategies linked to learning objectives and content standards. (7k)	The teacher varies her/his role in the instructional process, acting as instructor, facilitator, coach, and learner in response to the content and purposes of instruction. (7k; 8a; 8d; 8j; 8s)	The teacher serves as an advocate for learning by consciously selecting instructional roles to best meet the particular needs of learners as individuals and groups. (7k; 8d; 8j)
The teacher makes the learning objective(s) explicit and understandable to learners, providing a variety of graphic organizers, models, and representations for their learning. (8a; 8e; 8m)	The teacher offers learners choices about the topics and formats for major projects. S/he provides options for extensions and independent projects to challenge learners and to build their critical and creative thinking skills.(5a; 5o)	The teacher engages learners in the design and implementation of higher order learning experiences that are aligned with learning objectives, result in a variety of products and performances, and build on learners' interests and family and community resources. (8c)
As appropriate to the learning objective, the teacher prepares learners to use specific content-related processes and academic language. S/he also incorporates strategies to build group work skills. (4j)	The teacher engages individuals and groups of learners in identifying their strengths and specific needs for support and uses this information to adapt instruction. (7j)	The teacher scaffolds learners' ability to identify their own strengths and needs as learners and to take responsibility for setting individual learning goals, identifying and using strategies to achieve the goals, and seeking resources to support ongoing growth. (8c; 8l)
The teacher analyzes individual learner needs (e.g., language, thinking, processing) as well as patterns across groups of learners and uses instructional strategies to respond to those needs. (7j; 8b; 8l; 8p)	The teacher scaffolds student learning of academic language in the content area(s). (9l)	
The teacher integrates primary language resources into instruction.(8k; 8m; 8p)	The teacher supports learners' use of their primary language to facilitate the transfer of language skills and content knowledge from the primary language to the target language. (8k; 8m; 8p)	The teacher engages individual learners in recognizing how accommodations for learning modes, language proficiency, and special needs help them to be successful and/or in determining how the learner can best apply or adapt the accommodation. (8b; 8c; 8l; 8r)
The teacher seeks assistance in identifying general patterns of need in order to support language learners. (8k; 8m)		

Shift to increased ability to:

> **Expand teaching roles (e.g., instructor, facilitator, coach, audience) and employ them to tailor instruction and challenge all learners**

> **Use instruction to meet each learner's needs and empower learners as partners in designing and implementing higher order learning**

Developed through professional learning that will, for example:

BUILD KNOWLEDGE AND SKILL IN USE OF INSTRUCTIONAL STRATEGIES

❖ Observe a colleague who uses varied roles in teaching and debrief ways to match roles with instructional purpose
❖ Access structured input (e.g., workshops, in-person or online courses, webinars, social media) on second language acquisition and classroom supports for second language learners, including primary language supports
❖ Seek coaching to improve ability to support learner development of academic language

STRENGTHEN ANALYSIS AND REFLECTION ON USE OF INSTRUCTIONAL STRATEGIES

❖ Use grade-level or subject-area team meetings to target strategies that can differentiate support for learners with different needs
❖ Survey students to identify strengths and weaknesses in strategy repertoire and use feedback to adapt and expand range of strategies

EXPAND KNOWLEDGE AND SKILL IN USE OF INSTRUCTIONAL STRATEGIES

❖ Seek critique and suggestions for improvement in meeting each learner's needs from colleagues/coaches
❖ Work with colleagues and specialists to develop strategies that help learners take greater responsibility for self-advocacy
❖ Access structured input (e.g., workshops, in-person or online courses, webinars, social media) to refine strategies for engaging learners in the design and implementation of higher order learning

BUILD PROFESSIONAL COMMUNITY to advocate for the effective use of instructional strategies to support learners

❖ Develop a study group with colleagues to identify new resources and research to support high level learning for all learners
❖ Form an advocacy group to support the local school or district in building capacity to use instructional practices that make learning accessible for all learners

2. The teacher encourages learners to develop deep understanding of content areas, makes connections across content, and applies content knowledge in meaningful ways.

1	2	3
	And...	*And...*
The teacher helps learners use a variety of sources and tools, including technology, to access information related to an instructional objective. S/he helps students learn to evaluate the trustworthiness of sources and to organize the information in a way that would be clear to an authentic audience. (8g; 8j; 8n; 8o; 8r)	The teacher engages learners in using learning skills (e.g., critical and creative thinking skills, study skills, managing goals and time) and technology tools to access, interpret and apply knowledge that promotes learners' understanding of the learning objective(s). (8j; 8o; 8r)	The teacher engages learners in collaborative work to generate, synthesize, and communicate information useful to a specific audience. (8m; 8q; 8s)
The teacher poses questions that elicit learner thinking about information and concepts in the content areas as well as learner application of critical thinking skills such as inference making, comparing, and contrasting. (8f; 8g; 8q)	The teacher develops learners' abilities to pose questions that can guide individual and group exploration of concepts and their application. S/he engages learners in demonstrating multiple ways to explain a concept or perform a process related to an instructional objective(s). (8f; 8m; 8q)	The teacher collaborates with learners to create learning opportunities in which learners generate questions and design approaches for addressing them. (8f; 8s)
The teacher models the use of non-linguistic representations, concept mapping, and writing to show how learners can express their understanding of content area concepts and assigns work that allows the learners to practice doing so. (8e; 8m; 8q)	The teacher models higher order questioning skills related to content areas (e.g., generating hypotheses, taking multiple perspectives, using metacognitive processes) and engages learners in activities that develop these skills. (8f; 8l; 8m)	The teacher engages learners in connecting application of concepts from more than one content area to real world problems, community needs, and/or service learning. (5a)
The teacher develops learners' abilities to participate in respectful, constructive discussions of content in small and whole group settings. S/he establishes norms that include thoughtful listening, building on one another's ideas, and questioning for clarification. (8i; 8q)	The teacher engages learners in expanding their abilities to use group discussion to learn from each other and to build skills of interpretation, perspective taking, and connection-making grounded in content. (8i; 8m; 8q)	

Shift to increased ability to:

> **Use strategies to build deeper understanding and meaningful application of content and skills**

> **Engage learners in both higher order skills and self-directed learning opportunities that address authentic problems or issues**

Developed through professional learning that will, for example:

BUILD KNOWLEDGE AND SKILL TO TAKE LEARNERS DEEPER INTO CONTENT UNDERSTANDING AND APPLICATION

- ❖ Use structured input (e.g., workshops, in-person or online courses, webinars, social media) to develop higher order instructional strategies
- ❖ Observe teachers who use effective questioning in the content area and debrief with them
- ❖ Seek mentoring in use of group processes and cooperative learning to engage learners in higher order thinking

STRENGTHEN ANALYSIS AND REFLECTION ON USE OF STRATEGIES TO SUPPORT HIGHER ORDER LEARNING

- ❖ Use action research to examine how learners are using technology to access, interpret, and apply content knowledge
- ❖ Maintain a log of questions used in teaching to self-assess the variety, relevance, and rigor of questioning strategies

EXPAND KNOWLEDGE AND SKILLLS TO ENGAGE LEARNERS IN COLLABORATIVE INQUIRY

- ❖ Observe colleagues who are effective in building content area literacy skills and debrief
- ❖ Use structured input (e.g., workshops, in-person or online courses, webinars, social media) to learn approaches to develop learner autonomy in applying learning to real world contexts
- ❖ Use technology to connect and collaborate with educators in other communities and countries on authentic problems and issues
- ❖ Use reflective analysis strategies to build higher order thinking and self-direction

STRENGTHEN ANALYSIS AND REFLECTION ON THE IMPACT OF PARTICULAR HIGHER ORDER STRATEGIES

- ❖ Work with colleagues to implement and monitor the effect of strategies that support learner engagement and authentic problem solving
- ❖ Hold a focus group of colleagues to share challenges and successes in making higher order work with learners more collaborative

Are you Coachable?

Standard #9: Professional Learning and Ethical Practice

The teacher engages in ongoing professional learning and uses evidence to continually evaluate his/her practice, particularly the effects of his/her choices and actions on others (learners, families, other professionals, and the community), and adapts practice to meet the needs of each learner.

PERFORMANCES

9(a) The teacher engages in ongoing learning opportunities to develop knowledge and skills in order to provide all learners with engaging curriculum and learning experiences based on local and state standards.

9(b) The teacher engages in meaningful and appropriate professional learning experiences aligned with his/her own needs and the needs of the learners, school, and system.

9(c) Independently and in collaboration with colleagues, the teacher uses a variety of data (e.g., systematic observation, information about learners, research) to evaluate the outcomes of teaching and learning and to adapt planning and practice.

9(d) The teacher actively seeks professional, community, and technological resources, within and outside the school, as supports for analysis, reflection, and problem-solving.

9(e) The teacher reflects on his/her personal biases and accesses resources to deepen his/her own understanding of cultural, ethnic, gender, and learning differences to build stronger relationships and create more relevant learning experiences.

9(f) The teacher advocates, models, and teaches safe, legal, and ethical use of information and technology including appropriate documentation of sources and respect for others in the use of social media.

ESSENTIAL KNOWLEDGE

9(g) The teacher understands and knows how to use a variety of self-assessment and problem-solving strategies to analyze and reflect on his/her practice and to plan for adaptations/adjustments.

9(h) The teacher knows how to use learner data to analyze practice and differentiate instruction accordingly.

9(i) The teacher understands how personal identity, worldview, and prior experience affect perceptions and expectations, and recognizes how they may bias behaviors and interactions with others.

9(j) The teacher understands laws related to learners' rights and teacher responsibilities (e.g., for educational equity, appropriate education for learners with disabilities, confidentiality, privacy, appropriate treatment of learners, reporting in situations related to possible child abuse).

9(k) The teacher knows how to build and implement a plan for professional growth directly aligned with his/her needs as a growing professional using feedback from teacher evaluations and observations, data on learner performance, and school- and system-wide priorities.

CRITICAL DISPOSITIONS

9(l) The teacher takes responsibility for student learning and uses ongoing analysis and reflection to improve planning and practice.

9(m) The teacher is committed to deepening understanding of his/her own frames of reference (e.g., culture, gender, language, abilities, ways of knowing), the potential biases in these frames, and their impact on expectations for and relationships with learners and their families.

9(n) The teacher sees him/herself as a learner, continuously seeking opportunities to draw upon current education policy and research as sources of analysis and reflection to improve practice.

9(o) The teacher understands the expectations of the profession including codes of ethics, professional standards of practice, and relevant law and policy.

Progression for Standard #9: Professional Learning and Ethical Practice

The teacher engages in ongoing professional learning and uses evidence to continually evaluate his/her practice, particularly the effects of his/her choices and actions on others (learners, families, other professionals, and the community), and adapts practice to meet the needs of each learner.

1. The teacher engages in continuous professional learning to more effectively meet the needs of each learner.

1	2	3
	And...	*And...*
The teacher engages in structured individual and group professional learning opportunities to reflect on, identify, and address improvement needs and to enable him/her to provide all learners with engaging curriculum and learning experiences. (5r; 9a; 9b; 9k; 9n; 10f; 10t)	Based on reflection and other sources of feedback, the teacher takes responsibility for his/her self-assessment of practice and ongoing professional learning by seeking out and participating in professional learning experiences to address identified needs and areas of professional interest. (9a; 9b; 9k; 9n; 10t)	The teacher collaborates with colleagues to collectively reflect upon, analyze, and improve individual and collective practice to address learner, school, and professional needs. (9c; 9l; 10r)
The teacher completes professional learning processes and activities required by the state in order to meet re-certification or re-licensure requirements. (9b; 9k; 9nl; 10t)	The teacher engages in professional learning experiences that broaden her/his understanding of learner development and diverse needs in order to increase the level of personalization of practice. (9b; 9l)	The teacher engages and leads colleagues within the school/district/community in designing and implementing professional learning experiences that address identified needs to improve practice. (9b; 9n; 10f; 10i; 10t)
The teacher actively seeks professional, community, and technological resources, within and outside the school, as supports for analysis, reflection, and problem-solving. (9d)		

Shift to increased ability to:

Assume ownership and responsibility for ongoing professional learning connected to learner needs

Collaborate with colleagues to design and implement professional learning for self and others

Developed through professional learning that will, for example:

BUILD SKILLS ON HOW TO DEVELOP A PROFESSIONAL GROWTH PLAN

- ❖ Work with a coach/mentor to determine needs, set goals, and identify individually focused learning experiences to improve practice and student learning
- ❖ Share plan with key colleagues for feedback
- ❖ Examine own teacher evaluation data and identify strengths and areas for growth

STRENGTHEN ANALYSIS AND REFLECTION ON LEARNER NEEDS

- ❖ Keep journal on how teaching impacts student learning and identify potential areas of growth for self and learners
- ❖ Consult with grade level or content area team for professional learning options that can support learners

EXPAND SKILLS IN FACILITATING ADULT LEARNING

- ❖ Use structured input (e.g., workshops, in-person or online courses, webinars, social media) to develop facilitation/coaching skills for working with adult learners
- ❖ Seek feedback from mentor(s) to refine skill in working with adult learners

BUILD SKILL IN DESIGNING PROFESSIONAL LEARNING EXPERIENCES TO IMPROVE PRACTICE

- ❖ Use structured input (e.g., workshops, in-person or online courses, webinars, social media) to augment skill in developing targeted professional learning experiences for adult learners
- ❖ Use grade-level or subject area team meetings to seek feedback on planning appropriate collaborative professional learning experiences

2. The teacher uses evidence to continually evaluate the effects of his/her decisions on others and adapts professional practices to better meet learners' needs.

1	2	3
	And…	*And…*
The teacher observes and reflects upon learners' responses to instruction to identify areas and set goals for improved practice. (7p; 9c; 9g; 9l)	The teacher reflects on and analyzes a wide range of evidence (e.g., feedback from families, students and learners' peers) to evaluate the impact of instruction on individual learners and to set goals for improvement. (9c)	The teacher leads other educators in gathering, synthesizing and evaluating data to help them evaluate the effects of their individual and group decisions and actions on individuals and groups of learners, colleagues and community members and set goals for improvement. (9b; 9c; 9h; 9i; 9m; 10f; 10i; 10t)
The teacher seeks and reflects upon feedback from colleagues to evaluate the effects of her/his actions on learners, colleagues and community members. (9a; 9g; 9m; 9n)	The teacher collaborates with colleagues and others to give, receive and analyze feedback on the effects of their actions on learners, colleagues and community members and to apply it to improve practice. (9i; 10i)	The teacher supports and assists others to extend and refine their instructional practices and other professional behaviors to meet the needs of each learner. (9b; 9c; 9h; 9m; 10f; 10i; 10t)
The teacher gathers, synthesizes and analyzes a variety of data from sources inside and outside of the school to adapt instructional practices and other professional behaviors to better meet learners' needs. (9a; 9c; 9g; 9h; 9k; 9l; 9n)	The teacher collaborates with others to gather, synthesize and analyze data to adapt planning, instructional practices and other professional behavior to better meet individual learner needs. (9a; 9b; 9c; 9h; 9n; 10i; 10t)	

Shift to increased ability to:

> **Collaborate to analyze multiple sources of evidence and to evaluate the impact of instructional choices**

> **Guide, mentor, and coach others in synthesizing data, evaluating impact of practice, and setting goals for improvement**

Developed through professional learning that will, for example:

BUILD SKILL IN WORKING WITH DATA

- ❖ Use structured input (e.g., workshops, in-person or online courses, webinars, social media) on using data analysis for planning
- ❖ Use protocols to guide reflective analysis and evaluation of practice
- ❖ Work with colleagues to brainstorm ways to communicate and display data in a manner that is accessible and engaging for learners and parents

STRENGTHEN ANALYSIS AND REFLECTION ON GROWING SKILL IN ANALYSIS OF EVIDENCE

- ❖ Keep a journal of learner growth using varied forms of data
- ❖ Seek coaching to identify questions to guide reflection on data

ENHANCE SKILL IN WORKING WITH DATA ANALYSIS

- ❖ Pursue graduate work in quantitative and qualitative data analysis
- ❖ Work collaboratively with more experienced colleagues and get feedback and coaching on the use of data to guide coaching/mentoring

ENHANCE SKILL IN FACILITATING ADULT LEARNING

- ❖ Use structured input (e.g., workshops, in-person or online courses, webinars, social media) to develop facilitation/coaching skills for adult learners
- ❖ Engage a colleague as a mentor/coach and seek feedback on coaching practices and on the effectiveness of coaching to improve practice.

3. The teacher practices the profession in an ethical manner.

1	2	3
	And...	*And...*
The teacher acts in accordance with ethical codes of conduct and professional standards. (9o)	The teacher supports colleagues in exploring and making ethical decisions and adhering to professional standards. (9o)	The teacher collaborates with colleagues to deepen the learning community's awareness of the moral and ethical demands of professional practice. (9o; 10s; 10t)
The teacher complies with laws and policies related to learners' rights and teachers' responsibilities. (9j; 9o)	The teacher supports others in following the laws and policies related to learners' rights and teachers' responsibilities. (9j; 9o)	The teacher collaborates with others to evaluate how well laws and policies serve particular learners and advocates for changes in policies that would better meet learner needs. (9j; 9o; 10s; 10t)
The teacher accesses information and uses technology in safe, legal and ethical ways. (9f; 9j; 9o; 9o)	The teacher anticipates how information and technology might be used in unethical or illegal ways and takes steps to prevent the misuse of information and technology. (8o; 8r; 9f; 9o)	The teacher advocates for the safe, legal and ethical use of information and technology throughout the school community. (8r; 9f; 9o)
The teacher follows established rules and policies to ensure learners access information and technology in safe, legal and ethical ways. (9f)	The teacher uses a deepening understanding of cultural, ethnic, gender and learning differences to reflect on the needs of learners and to design and implement strategies to better meet the needs of learners.(9e; 9m)	The teacher assists others in exploring how personal identity can affect perceptions and assists them in reflecting upon their personal biases in order to act more fairly. (4q; 9e; 9i; 9m)
The teacher recognizes how his/her identity affects perceptions and biases and reflects on the fairness and equity of his/her decisions. (4q; 9e; 9m)		The teacher shares resources and strategies with others to help them better understand the cultural, ethnic, gender and learning differences of learners and their communities. (9e; 10i)
The teacher accesses resources to deepen his/her understanding of the cultural, ethnic, gender and learning differences among learners and their communities. (9e)		The teacher uses knowledge of learners' cultural, ethnic, gender and learning differences to advocate for changes in policy and practice that better address the needs of learners. (9o)
The teacher reflects on the needs of individual learners and how well they are being addressed, seeking to build support for all learners. (9l)		

Shift to increased ability to:

> **Support others in applying ethical and professional practice to better meet learner needs**

> **Serve as advocate, guide, and coach in addressing ethical issues**

Developed through professional learning that will, for example:

BUILD SKILL IN RECOGNIZING AND ADDRESSING ETHICAL ISSUES

- ❖ Use structured input (e.g., workshops, in-person or online courses, webinars, social media) to develop ability to articulate and apply ethical principles in professional practice
- ❖ Organize collegial book discussion group to explore issues of equity and ethics in education
- ❖ Study professional codes of ethics and professional standards and share findings with colleagues

STRENGTHEN ANALYSIS AND REFLECTION ON ETHICAL DILEMMAS

- ❖ Engage colleagues, mentors, and specialists in identifying ethical issues related to technology in teaching and learning and address potential challenges
- ❖ Organize a book club about possible approaches to address cultural, ethnic, gender, and learning differences that promote equity

BUILD SKILLS IN DIALOGUE

- ❖ Use structured input (e.g., workshops, in-person or online courses, webinars, social media) to develop skills in listening, reflection, and synthesis in order to facilitate dialogue and debate about ethical issues
- ❖ Form book study group with colleagues focused on issues of dialogue and community building
- ❖ Seek coaching on the development of dialogic skills related to ethical and equitable practice

CREATE LEARNING COMMUNITIES AROUND ETHICAL ISSUES

- ❖ Organize a group with colleagues to identify and evaluate ethical issues at school or district level
- ❖ Share resources (books, videos, websites) with colleagues and engage in discussion of ethical issues and potential steps to address the issues

Standard #10: Leadership and Collaboration

The teacher seeks appropriate leadership roles and opportunities to take responsibility for student learning, to collaborate with learners, families, colleagues, other school professionals, and community members to ensure learner growth, and to advance the profession.

PERFORMANCES

10(a) The teacher takes an active role on the instructional team, giving and receiving feedback on practice, examining learner work, analyzing data from multiple sources, and sharing responsibility for decision making and accountability for each student's learning.

10(b) The teacher works with other school professionals to plan and jointly facilitate learning on how to meet diverse needs of learners.

10(c) The teacher engages collaboratively in the school-wide effort to build a shared vision and supportive culture, identify common goals, and monitor and evaluate progress toward those goals.

10(d) The teacher works collaboratively with learners and their families to establish mutual expectations and ongoing communication to support learner development and achievement.

10(e) Working with school colleagues, the teacher builds ongoing connections with community resources to enhance student learning and well being.

10(f) The teacher engages in professional learning, contributes to the knowledge and skill of others, and works collaboratively to advance professional practice.

10(g) The teacher uses technological tools and a variety of communication strategies to build local and global learning communities that engage learners, families, and colleagues.

10(h) The teacher uses and generates meaningful research on education issues and policies.

10(i) The teacher seeks appropriate opportunities to model effective practice for colleagues, to lead professional learning activities, and to serve in other leadership roles.

10(j) The teacher advocates to meet the needs of learners, to strengthen the learning environment, and to enact system change.

10(k) The teacher takes on leadership roles at the school, district, state, and/or national level and advocates for learners, the school, the community, and the profession.

ESSENTIAL KNOWLEDGE

10(l) The teacher understands schools as organizations within a historical, cultural, political, and social context and knows how to work with others across the system to support learners.

10(m) The teacher understands that alignment of family, school, and community spheres of influence enhances student learning and that discontinuity in these spheres of influence interferes with learning.

10(n) The teacher knows how to work with other adults and has developed skills in collaborative interaction appropriate for both face-to-face and virtual contexts.

10(o) The teacher knows how to contribute to a common culture that supports high expectations for student learning.

CRITICAL DISPOSITIONS

10(p) The teacher actively shares responsibility for shaping and supporting the mission of his/her school as one of advocacy for learners and accountability for their success.

10(q) The teacher respects families' beliefs, norms, and expectations and seeks to work collaboratively with learners and families in setting and meeting challenging goals.

10(r) The teacher takes initiative to grow and develop with colleagues through interactions that enhance practice and support student learning.

10(s) The teacher takes responsibility for contributing to and advancing the profession.

10(t) The teacher embraces the challenge of continuous improvement and change.

Progression for Standard #10: Leadership and Collaboration

The teacher seeks appropriate leadership roles and opportunities to take responsibility for student learning, to collaborate with learners, families, colleagues, other school professionals, and community members to ensure learner growth, and to advance the profession.

1. The teacher collaborates with learners, families, colleagues, other school professionals, and community members to ensure learner growth.

1	2	3
	And...	*And...*
The teacher participates on the instructional team(s) and uses advice and support from colleagues to meet the needs of all learners. (10a; 10n; 10r)	The teacher collaborates with colleagues on the instructional team(s) to probe data and seek and offer feedback on practices that support learners. (10a; 10b; 10f; 10n; 10o; 10r)	The teacher brings innovative practices that meet learning needs to the instructional team(s) and supports colleagues in their use and in analyzing their effectiveness. (10a; 10f; 10i; 10k; 10s)
The teacher participates in school-wide efforts to implement a shared vision and contributes to a supportive culture. (10a; 10c; 10n; 10o; 10p; 10r)	The teacher engages in school-wide decision making with colleagues to identify common goals, and monitor and evaluate progress toward those goals. (10a; 10c; 10l; 10n; 10o; 10p; 10r)	The teacher advocates for continuous evaluation and improvement of the school-wide vision, mission and goals to ensure alignment with learner needs. (10b; 10c; 10k; 10l; 10p; 10s; 10t)
The teacher elicits information about learners and their experiences from families and communities and uses this ongoing communication to support learner development and growth. (10d; 10m; 10q)	The teacher works with families to develop mutual expectations for learner performance and growth and how to support it. (10d; 10g; 10m; 10n; 10o; 10q)	The teacher supports colleagues in developing increasingly effective communication and collaboration with diverse families and community members. (8p; 10a; 10d; 10e; 10f; 10g; 10k; 10m; 10n; 10q; 10r)
The teacher uses technology and other forms of communication to develop collaborative relationships with learners, families, colleagues and the local community. (8h; 10d; 10g)	Working with school colleagues, the teacher connects families with community resources that enhance student learning and family well-being. (9l; 10b; 10d; 10e; 10m; 10n; 10o; 10r)	The teacher advocates in the school and community to meet the needs of learners and their families, and to strengthen the community/ school culture for learning. (10d; 10e; 10k;10l; 10m; 10o; 10p; 10q; 10t)
	The teacher structures interactions between learners and their local and global peers around projects that engage them in deep learning. (5a)	The teacher works collaboratively across the learning community of learners, families, teachers, administrators, and others to support enhancement of student learning, for example by showcasing learner work physically and/or virtually for critique and celebration. (10a; 10d;10e; 10k; 10m; 10n; 10q)
	The teacher builds ongoing communities of support for student learning, through exchanging information, advice and resources with families and colleagues. (9l; 10m; 10n; 10o; 10q)	

Shift to increased ability to:

Deepen collaborative engagement with colleagues, learners, and learners' families

Engage in advocacy in varied collaborative contexts

Developed through professional learning that will, for example:

BUILD SKILLS IN WORKING COLLABORATIVELY with learners, colleagues, and communities

- ❖ Seek feedback and mentoring to improve active listening, empathy, reframing, and perspective taking
- ❖ Form a study group to read and reflect on processes that can improve collaboration
- ❖ Use technology to build collaborative skills locally and globally

STRENGTHEN ANALYSIS AND REFLECTION ON STRENGTHS AND WEAKNESSES IN COLLABORATIVE WORK

- ❖ Seek feedback from learners on use of strategies to support their collaboration with local and global peers
- ❖ Keep a reflective journal on insights gained from interaction with colleagues and community members

BUILD PROFESSIONAL AND COMMUNITY CONNECTIONS in support of learner growth

- ❖ Shadow a community member/colleague who demonstrates advocacy for learners
- ❖ Participate in a professional organization workshop to build specific leadership skills (e.g., evaluation and problem-solving)
- ❖ Seek mentoring in ways to support colleagues in working with diverse families

BUILD SKILLS IN IDENTIFYING HOW INNOVATION IN ONE AREA CAN IMPACT OTHER AREAS

- ❖ Read current literature on organizational development and leadership and explore how to apply these strategies to schools and districts
- ❖ Form a technology think tank with colleagues to explore uses of new technologies for instructional purposes

2. The teacher seeks appropriate leadership roles and opportunities to take responsibility for student learning and to advance the profession.

1	2	3
	And...	*And...*
The teacher leads in his/her own classroom, assuming responsibility for and directing student learning toward high expectations. (9l)	The teacher works with other school professionals to plan and jointly facilitate ongoing learning to better meet diverse needs of learners. (8p; 10a; 10b; 10n; 10r)	The teacher models effective instructional strategies for colleagues, leads professional learning activities, and serves in other leadership roles. (10i; 10k; 10n; 10r; 10s)
The teacher makes practice transparent by sharing plans and inviting observation and feedback. (10r)	The teacher contributes to the growth of others through mentoring, feedback and/or sharing of practice. (10k; 10r)	The teacher motivates colleagues to consider leadership roles. (10k)
The teacher works to improve practice through action research. (10h)	The teacher collaborates with colleagues to jointly conduct action research and share results with the learning community. (10a; 10k; 10n; 10r)	The teacher works independently and collaboratively to generate research and use it as a way to impact education issues and policies. (10a;10h; 10k; 10n; 10r; 10s)
	The teacher contributes to establishing and maintaining a climate of trust, critical reflection, and inclusivity where diverse perspectives are welcomed in addressing challenges. (8p; 10k; 10n; 10o; 10p)	The teacher advocates for learners, the school, the community, and the profession through leadership roles at the school, district, state, and/or national levels. (10e; 10k; 10p; 10s)

Shift to increased ability to:

Assume varied leadership roles

Coach and encourage others, generate research that can influence policy, and advocate through leadership roles

Developed through professional learning that will, for example:

BUILD LEADERSHIP SKILLS

❖ Use structured processes (e.g., workshops, in-person or online courses, webinars, social media) to develop skills related to team work, mentoring, and group facilitation

❖ Join colleagues in a book study related to how to build inclusive structures at the school level

STRENGTHEN ANALYSIS AND REFLECTION ON LEADERSHIP SKILLS

❖ Video record self in group situation, analyze interaction, and set goals for improvement

❖ Seek feedback from critical friend(s) on application of leadership skills

BUILD SKILLS TO CONDUCT AND DISSEMINATE RESEARCH

❖ Use structured input (e.g., workshops, in-person or online courses, webinars, social media) to learn and practice research and presentation skills

❖ Join an online discussion group that explores best practices for how to address various school-level issues

STRENGTHEN ANALYSIS AND REFLECTION ON VARIED LEADERSHIP ROLES

❖ Shadow a leader in the profession and debrief the experience

❖ Explore entry pathways to taking leadership roles in schools, districts, or professional organizations

❖ Use structured input (e.g., workshops, in-person or online courses, webinars, social media) to explore theory and strategies around how to support adult learning

Glossary of Terms

This glossary includes only those terms that are helpful to understanding how the InTASC standards have changed, particularly where new emphases or new understandings are implicated.

Academic Language

Academic language, tied to specific subject area disciplines, captures--through vocabulary, grammar, and organizational strategies--the complex ideas, higher order thinking processes, and abstract concepts of the discipline. It is the language used in classrooms, textbooks, and formal presentations in a subject area and differs in structure and vocabulary from everyday spoken English.

Assessment

Assessment is the productive process of monitoring, measuring, evaluating, documenting, reflecting on, and adjusting teaching and learning to ensure students reach high levels of achievement. Assessment systems need to include both formative and summative assessment processes, aligned with instructional and curricular goals and objectives. Formative assessment findings should be used as a continuous feedback loop to improve teaching and learning. Summative assessment results should be used to make final decisions about gains in knowledge and skills.

Formative Assessment

Formative assessment is a process used by teachers and learners that provides a continuous stream of evidence of learner growth, empowering teachers to adjust instruction and learners to adjust learning to improve student achievement. Formative assessment requires clear articulation and communication of intended instructional outcomes and criteria for success, ongoing descriptive feedback, the use of assessment evidence to make adjustments to teaching and learning, self- and peer-assessment that promote learner awareness of growth and needed improvement, and a partnership between teachers and learners which holds both parties accountable for learner achievement and success.

Summative Assessment

Summative assessment is the process of certifying learning at the culmination of a given period of time to evaluate the extent to which instructional objectives have been met. Examples of summative assessment include end-of-unit tests, final exams, semester exams, portfolios, capstone projects, performance demonstrations, state-mandated tests, the National Assessment of Educational Progress (NAEP), and accountability measures (e.g., Adequate Yearly Progress or AYP).

Collaboration

Collaboration is a style of interaction between individuals engaged in shared decision-making as they work toward a common goal. Individuals who collaborate have equally valued personal or professional resources to contribute and they share decision-making authority and accountability for outcomes.

Content Knowledge

Content knowledge includes not only a particular set of information, but also the framework for organizing information and processes for working with it. The traditional definition of content knowledge has been extended in these standards in three ways. First, it incorporates the notion of "pedagogical content knowledge," which blends content and effective instructional strategies for teaching particular subject matter, including appropriate representations and explanations. Second, it includes connections to other disciplines and the development of new, interdisciplinary areas of focus such as civic literacy, environmental literacy, and global awareness. Third, the notion of content knowledge is further extended to include cross-disciplinary skills as tools of inquiry and means to probe content deeply and apply it in real world contexts.

Reference Chart of Key Cross-Cutting Themes in Updated InTASC Standards

This chart shows where in the text of the standards certain key themes are referenced, demonstrating how they have been integrated across the document. In some instances, the key theme is not explicit but can be inferred.

Theme	Knowledge	Disposition	Performance
*Collaboration	3(j), 3(k), 3(i), 5(p), 7(m), 10(l), 10(n)	1(k), 3(n), 3(o), 3(p), 6(q), 6(s), 7(o), 9(l), 10(q), 10(r)	1(c), 3(a), 3(b), 3(c), 3(e), 3(h), 6(c), 7(a), 7(e), 8(b), 8(c), 9(a-d), 10(a-g)
*Communication	3(l), 3(j), 5(n), 6(l), 6(n), 6(o), 8(m), 10(n)	3(q), 3(r), 6(q), 6(s), 8(q)	3(c), 3(e), 3(f), 3(h), 5(e), 6(d), 6(e), 8(h), 8(i), 10(g)
*Creativity/Innovation	5(l), 5(o), 8(j), 8(m)	3(p), 5(s)	5(d), 5(f), 5(g), 8(i), 9(f)
*Critical thinking, problem solving	4(j), 4(k), 4(l), 5(i), 5(m), 8(j), 8(l), 9(g)	4(p), 4(r), 5(q)	4(b), 4(c), 4(d), 4(e), 4(h), 5(a), 5(b), 5(d), 5(f), 5(g), 6(f), 8(f), 8(g), 8(i), 9(d)
Cultural competence	1(g), 2(g), 2(j), 2(k), 3(i), 4(k), 4(m), 7(i), 8(k), 9(i)	4(o), 8(t), 9(m)	2(d), 3(f), 5(h), 7(c), 9(e)
English language learners	1(g), 2(i), 2(j), 6(p), 7(m), 8(m)	2(o), 6(u)	2(d), 2(e), 4(i), 6(h), 7(e)
Families/Communities	2(j), 2(k), 10(m)	1(k), 2(m), 3(n), 7(o), 9(m), 10(q)	1(c), 2(d), 3(a), 8(c), 9(b), 10(c), 10(d), 10(e), 10(g), 10(k)
Individual differences	1(d-g), 2(g), 2(h), 2(j), 2(k), 3(l), 4(l), 4(m), 6(k), 6(l), 6(m), 6(o), 6(p), 7(i-m), 8(k), 8(l), 9(g), 9(h), 9(i), 9(j)	1(h), 1(i), 1(k), 2(l), 2(m), 2(n), 2(o), 4(r), 6(q), 6(s), 6(u), 7(n), 7(q), 8(p), 8(s), 9(m)	1(a), 1(b), 2(a-f), 2(h), 3(d), 3(f), 4(a), 4(d), 4(e), 4(f), 4(g), 6(c), 6(d), 6(g), 6(h), 6(i), 7(b), 7(c), 7(d-f), 8(a), 8(b), 8(d), 8(e), 8(f), 9(a), 9(c), 9(e), 10(a). 10(b)
Interdisciplinary themes	5(j)	5(q-s)	5(c), 5(b), 5(e)
Leadership	1(c), 3(k), 5(p), 7(l), 7(m), 8(l), 8(n), 9(i), 9(j), 10(l-o)	1(j), 3(n), 4(p), 5(q), 6(r), 6(v), 7(o), 7(p), 8(s), 9(m), 9(n), 10(p-t)	2(f), 3(a), 3(c), 3(d), 4(g), 5(d), 5(g), 6(c), 6(e), 6(f), 7(a), 7(e), 8(c), 8(d), 9(a-f), 10(a-k)
*Multiple perspectives	5(i), 5(j), 5(n), 5(p), 9(i), 7(h), 10(l), 10(m)	4(p), 5(r), 6(t)	2(d), 3(e), 4(b), 5(a), 5(b), 5(d), 5(e), 5(g)
Professional learning	6(j-p), 7(f), 7(k), 8(k), 8(n), 8(o), 9(g-k)	4(o), 4(p), 4(q), 5(q), 5(r), 6(t), 8(p), 9(l-o), 10(r), 10(s), 10(t)	6(a), 6(c), 6(g), 6(i), 8(g), 9(a-f), 10(f), 10(h)
Student-directed learning	3(i), 3(k), 5(m), 6(m)	3(n), 3(o), 3(p), 6(q), 6(s), 10(q)	3(b), 3(c), 5(d), 5(f), 6(f), 8(b), 8(c)
Teacher responsibility	3(m), 5(l), 9(j), 9(k), 10(o)	1(j), 4(o), 4(q), 5(r), 6(r), 6(t), 6(u), 6(v), 7(p), 9(l-o), 10(p), 10(r), 10(s)	3(c), 3(g), 5(h), 9(e), 9(f)
*Technology	3(j), 3(m), 5(k), 5(l), 7(k), 8(n), 8(o), 10(n)	8(q), 8(r)	3(g), 3(h), 4(g), 5(c), 6(i), 8(g), 9(d), 9(f), 10(e), 10(g)
Use of data to support learning	5(k), 6(j-p), 7(l), 8(n), 8(o), 9(g), 9(h), 9(k)	6(q-v), 7(q), 8(s), 9(l)	2(d), 5(c), 5(f), 6(a-i), 8(b), 8(d), 8(g), 9(c), 9(f), 10(a-c)

Cross-disciplinary skills

InTASC Model Core Teaching Standards Update Committee

Mary Diez, Co-Chair
Dean, School of Education, Alverno College

Peter McWalters, Co-Chair
Commissioner, Rhode Island Department of Education (retired)

Kathleen Paliokas, Director
InTASC, Council of Chief State School Officers

David Paradise, Senior Associate
InTASC, Council of Chief State School Officers

- Richard Allan, Vice President, Evaluation Systems group of Pearson

- Katherine Bassett, Director, Educator Relations Group, Educational Testing Service (Teacher of the Year – New Jersey)

- Victoria Chamberlain, Executive Director, Oregon Teacher Standards and Practices Commission

- Pamela Coleman, Director of Teacher Education and Licensure, Kansas State Department of Education

- Lynne Cook, Professor of Special Education and Director of the EdD in Educational Leadership at California State University, Dominguez Hills

- Manuel Cox, Lead Teacher, Engineering Academy for Student Excellence (EASE), American High School (NBCT)

- Nadene Davidson, Interim Head, Department of Teaching, University of Northern Iowa (NBCT)

- Sydnee Dickson, Director, Teaching and Learning, Utah State Office of Education

- Karen Huffman, Assistant Superintendent, Division of Educator Quality, West Virginia Department of Education

- Maria Hyler, Assistant Professor, University of Maryland, College Park (NBCT)

- Susan Johnsen, Professor in the Department of Educational Psychology and Director of the PhD Program, School of Education, Baylor University

- Carlene Kirkpatrick, Instructional Coach, DeKalb County School System (NBCT)

- Jean Miller, Consultant, Council of Chief State School Officers

- Antoinette Mitchell, Interim Dean, School of Education, Trinity Washington University

- Gwen Wallace Nagel, Director, Iowa Learning Online, Iowa Department of Education

- Richelle Patterson, Senior Policy Analyst, Teacher Quality Department, National Education Association

- Irving Richardson, Coordinator for Public Education and School Support NEA-NH (Teacher of the Year - Maine)

- Maria del Carmen Salazar, Assistant Professor, Curriculum and Instruction Morgridge College of Education, University of Denver

- Theodore Small, 5th grade teacher, Clark County School District, Nevada

- Afi Y. Wiggins, PhD Candidate, Research Statistics and Evaluation, Curry School of Education, University of Virginia

NBCT – National Board Certified Teacher

InTASC Learning Progressions Drafting Committee

Mary Diez, Co-Chair
Dean, School of Education, Alverno College

Kathleen Paliokas, Director
InTASC, Council of Chief State School Officers

- Katherine Bassett, Director, Educator Relations Group, Educational Testing Service (Teacher of the Year – New Jersey)

- Dan Conley, Senior Account Representative, Evaluation Systems group of Pearson

- Karen Huffman, Assistant Superintendent, Division of Educator Quality, West Virginia Department of Education

- Carlene Kirkpatrick, Instructional Coach, DeKalb County School System (NBCT)

- Jean Miller, Consultant, former Director of InTASC, Council of Chief State School Officers

- Antoinette Mitchell, Deputy Assistant Superintendent, Postsecondary Education and Workforce Readiness, Office of the State Superintendent of Education (OSSE), Washington, DC

- Irving Richardson, Coordinator for Public Education and School Support NEA-NH (Teacher of the Year - Maine)

- Maria del Carmen Salazar, Assistant Professor, Curriculum and Instruction Morgridge College of Education, University of Denver

- Theodore Small, 5th grade teacher, Clark County School District, Nevada

- Kendyll Stansbury, Stanford Center for Assessment, Learning, and Equity (SCALE), Stanford University

NBCT – National Board Certified Teacher

Made in the USA
Monee, IL
19 August 2021

Literacy Foundations for English Learners